a river of love

a. kaggwa lubega

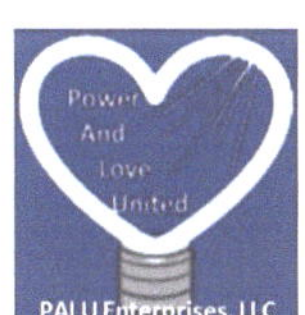

Published by PALU Enterprises, LLC
Rockville, Maryland
2016

Andereya Kaggwa Mawesano Lubega

ISBN 13: 978-0-9862322-2-0
ISBN 10: 098623222X

CONTENTS

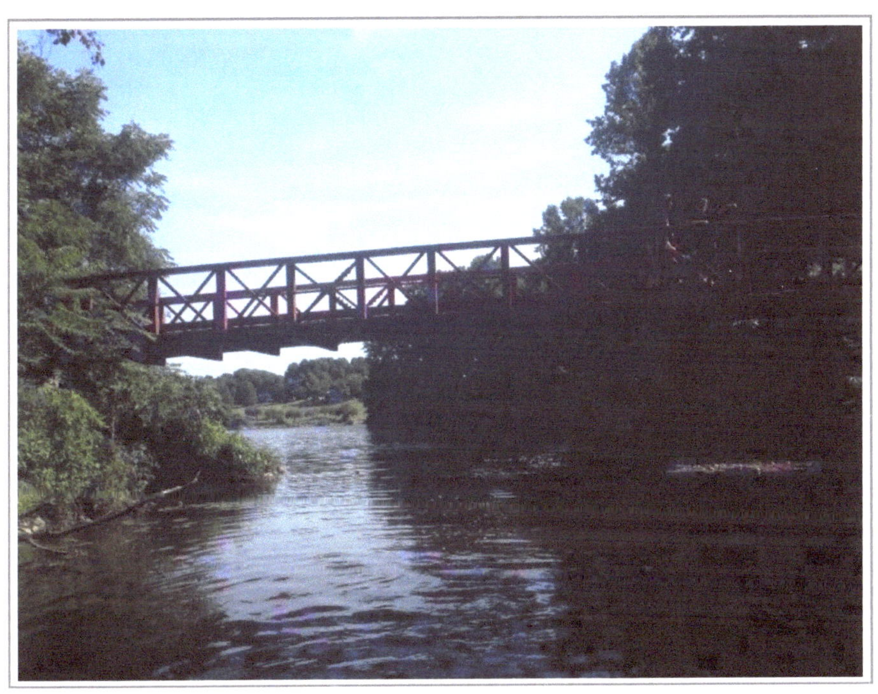

"I have known rivers come to life in human form. This was one of them. His name was Andereya Kaggwa Mawesano Lubega while he roamed this plane. Now, well, he's elsewhere. He touched many people, spoke life to many souls, refreshed thirsty spirits, and propagated love."

Steven Gaskill

PREFACE

When the author transitioned to new life, he left much of himself with us. We chant the prayers and affirmations he taught us. We dance the dances he danced with us and sing the songs he sang with us. We hear his voice of love constantly reminding us what is of utmost importance in this life. We find ourselves being kind, tolerant and accommodating, largely, because of what he demonstrated to us. However, his lifetime gifts do not end there. We can tap into his heartfelt wishes through the personal messages he sent us or see his smile and hear his voice online and we know that he lives on.

This work is presented almost exactly as Kaggwa prepared it. Its cover was designed using lower case font to represent the humility with which he lived his life. The photos he captured, mostly at SRF Mother Center, seem to fit miraculously. There are a few from our family albums that also work well. One in particular looks as if it holds a very special, and even mystical, secret. We would love to hear from readers who notice it.

The appendix is a poem that he might have written to his inner child (represented in the accompanying photo by a doll he bought many years ago to remind himself) or, perhaps, imagining that God was speaking to him. Whatever the case, it is such a beautiful expression that we thought it was well worth sharing.

Our guess is that this entire work will touch many people in unimaginable ways just as has its author. Thank God for the wonderful and infinite gift of Andereya Kaggwa Mawesano Lubega!

FOREWORD

Kaggwa gave me the manuscript for this book many years ago. I skimmed through the poems, told him how nice they are, and filed the manuscript away with my own work as we tried to figure out how to go about publishing. 2006. Ten years ago. Shortly before Kaggwa began New Life, I was going through some boxes and saw the manuscript as he was walking by and gave it to him. He took it and kept going. I had no idea what he did with it.

Once he left us, there was a dire need to harness whatever I could of him. As I poured over, copied and categorized his notes, photographs, letters and tried to figure how I could best honor him, I remembered the manuscript and regretted having returned it to him. Weeks passed, then months and, one day when I was cleaning out some boxes, I found the manuscript that I had returned to my son.

I started typing the poems into my computer; as I did so, it was as if I was reading them for the first time. It was as if Kaggwa was speaking, pouring out his heart and soul concerning every part of his existence.

His poems are candid, raw, and so true. I resisted the urge to ponder them to ask how, why or what part I played in any of this often turbulent expression of the many aspects yet single face of love.

A lifetime of questioning things I am told, things I experience, and things I feel has led me to one conclusion. All things God.

Awestruck and with deep deep gratitude, I bask in His unbridled and incessant love engulfing me. *P.B. Lubega*

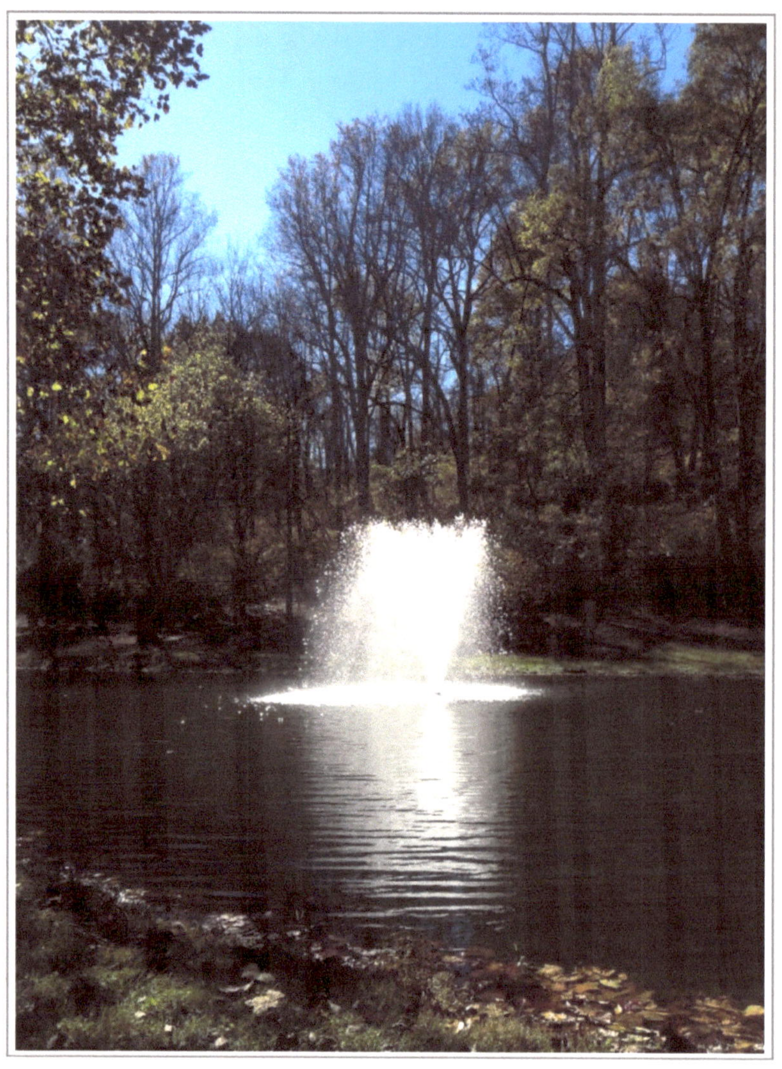

DEDICATION

This book, "A River of Love", is dedicated to all people of the earth.

We are of one blood, the essence of which is love. No matter where we are or what we do or have done, no matter what our experiences in this ephemeral world, the bottom line is that life is about love.

Not just any love but, divine, unconditional love. That love is the lost treasure, the fountain of youth, the bliss, the never-ending satisfaction that we seek outside of ourselves in all our experiences. It is actually the essence of who and what we are.

We simply have to turn within and notice, recognize, acknowledge and feel its presence.

My wish for all humanity is that we find that love and give it to all. Life is not easy. Love is not easy, but it is right and we all aspire towards it.

Love is our nature. Many of us are, to a greater or lesser extent, out of touch with that nature. We must become one with it again. We must re-establish the state of our hearts. We must merge with that which we are. Is there any other thing that we can long to be besides that which we are? Nothing would be of value to us for long except that state that is our native home.

The result of being out of touch with ourselves is pain. No one wants pain and suffering. What we do want is lasting joy and happiness, the exact result of being in touch with our real selves-of being in touch with love.

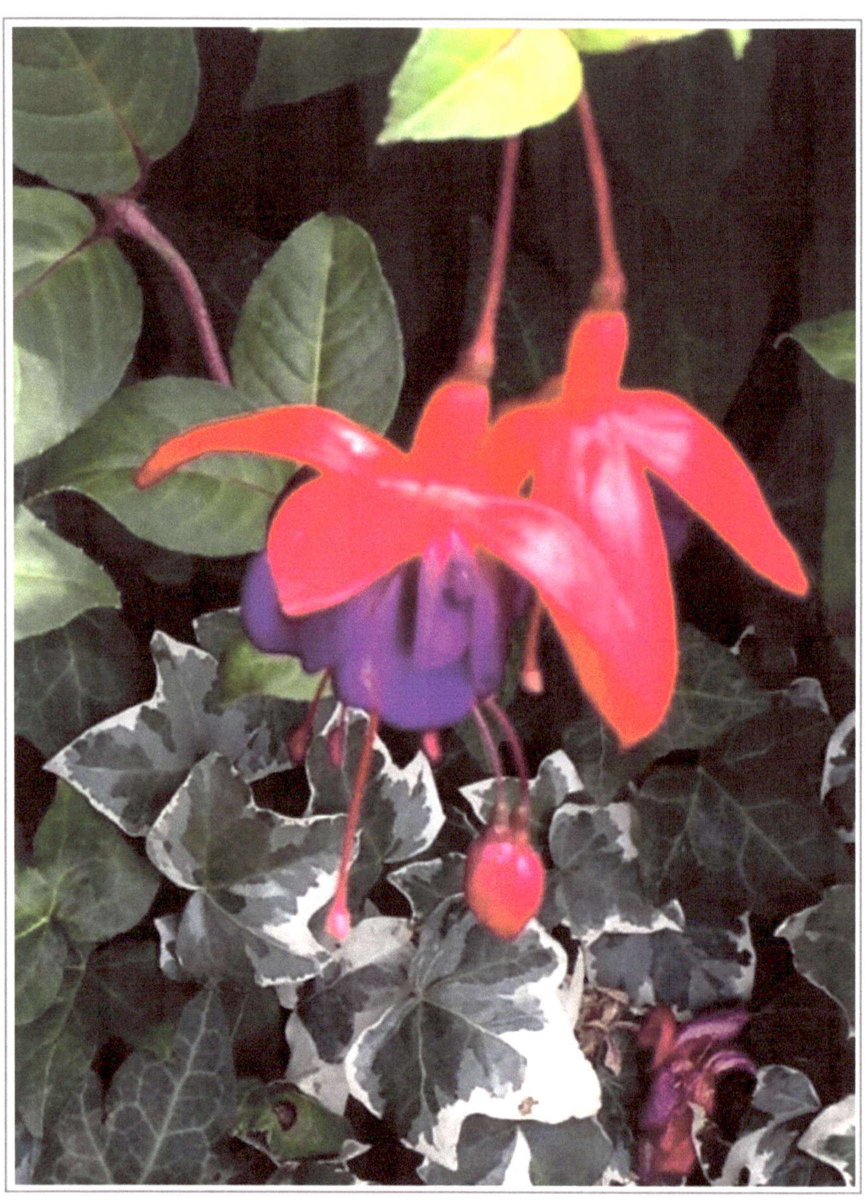

YOU A GEM

You are a gem of inestimable value:
A rare gift that cannot be replaced.

You are neither better nor worse than anyone else.

You are unique and as such share a common bond with humanity- your would-be brothers, sisters, mothers, fathers, daughters and sons.

You need do nothing and nothing you do can take away from your value.

You are an eternal light: a beacon, a lighthouse bringing the positive rays of sunshine presence to this drama of life.

You are so powerful, so free, so unfettered by anything.

You are love's embrace: the warmth the babe feels in its mother's arms, the pure feeling the mother feels as she effortlessly nurtures her new-born babe.

Nothing brings you down. Whatever touches you becomes a part of that love: it cannot help but do so.

That touch is enough to inundate it immediately, to absorb it, to permeate it entirely and pull it into the circle of your love.

So powerful is your love that all it takes is one step close to you and the magnetic power of that force draws everything in.
So powerful, so bright, so glorious are you that there is nowhere that you can hide....

A RIVER OF LOVE

I thought of You
And my heart poured forth
A river of Love

I forgot You
Or rather let You take second place
And the river dried up.
I lived in desperate thirst for Love
Not realizing that Thine All-Thirst-Quenching Presence
Was right within me.

I searched for Your joy and satisfaction
In the empty wells of material hope and human love.
Finally, when I saw all these wells are dry
And remembered and realized
That You should have first place
In my heart...

I thought of You
And my heart poured forth
A River of Love.

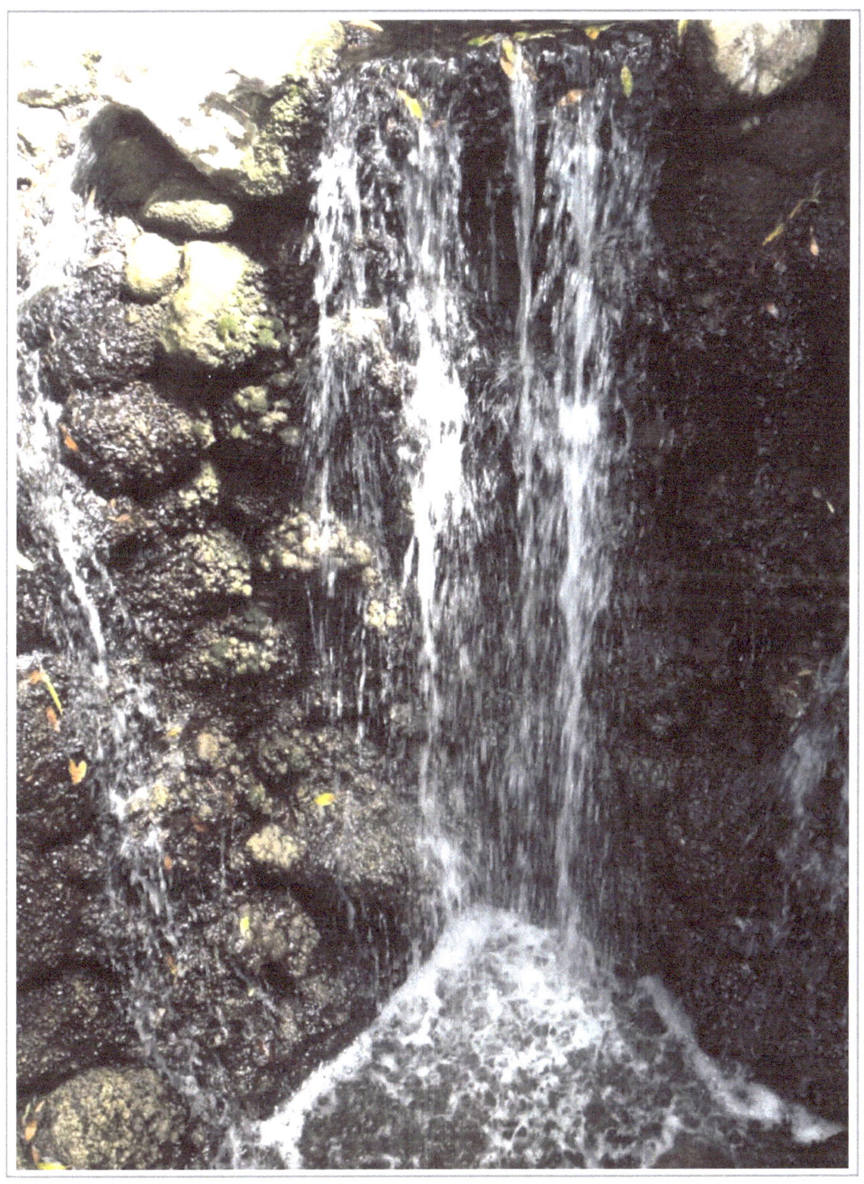

A SIMPLE WISH

I wish my mind
To think of Thee
To think of Thee
Oh constantly

Though ages come
And ages go
My thought of Thee
Shan't cease to flow

Like a river that
Never ends
My dear, my dearest
My best of friends

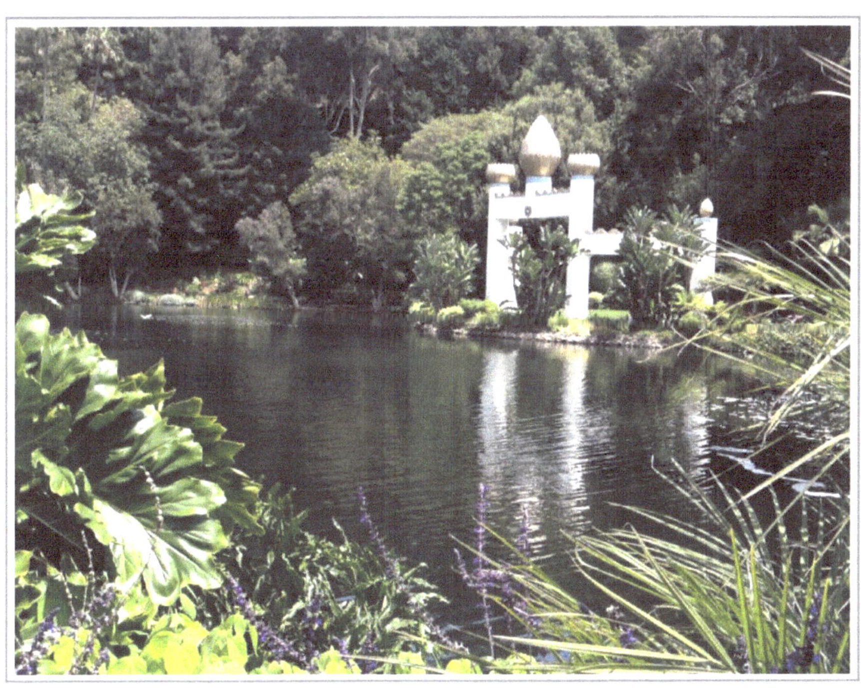

FRIEND

Oh my beautiful
Wonderful One
Who glows brighter
Than any sun
Whose compassion
Sees no limit, no end
Who's unconditionally
An eternal friend

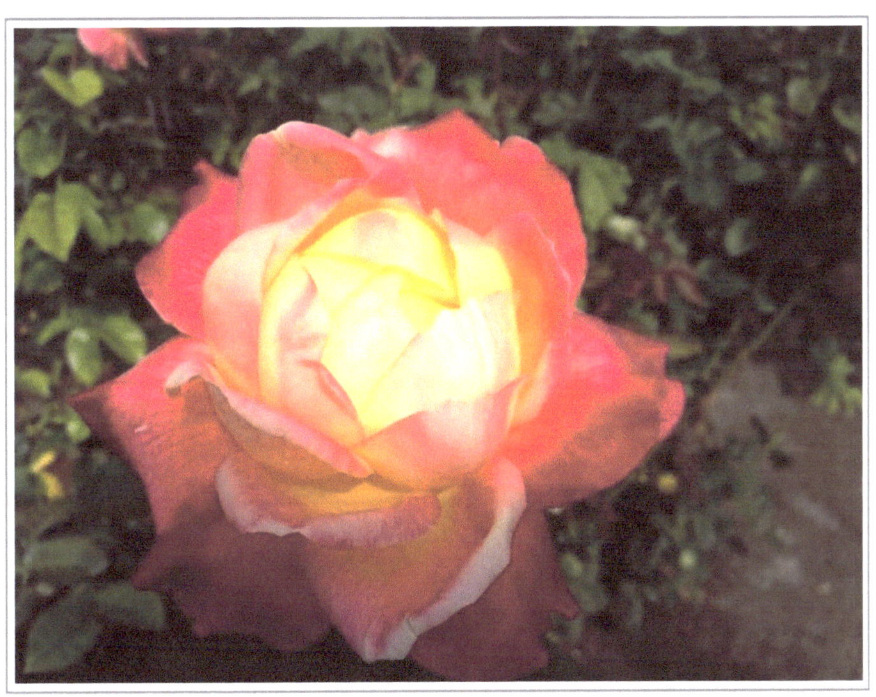

YOU ALONE

I know nothing
Except that I love You
I desire nothing
Except to love You more
I seek nothing
But to find You
Dancing Your eternal dance
Of happiness in my heart

I am nothing
Without You
I am nothing
Without Your love
I do nothing
For Your strength is
My support
I am nothing
Because
You are everything

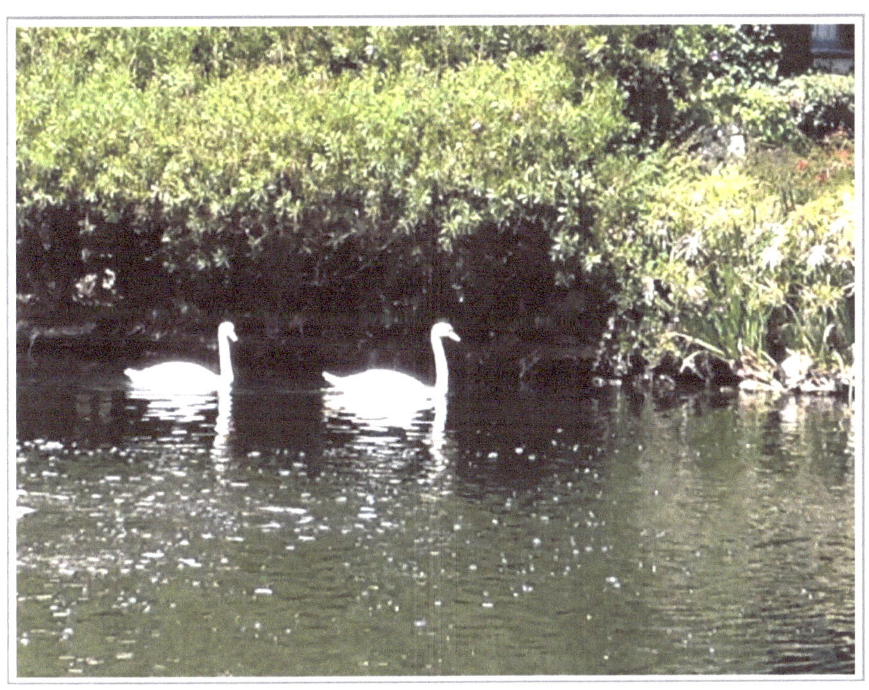

AS I AM

As I am,
I lie humbly at Thy feet
To receive Thy blessing, guidance and protection.

As I am,
I place the crumbs
Of my imperfect devotions
At Thy feet
That Thou may take them and expand them
Into an ever purer unselfish love

As I am,
I seek, in my daily life,
To remember Thee
To do Thy will in my life to the best of my ability
To remember that Thou art in charge.

As I am
I remind myself to never forget
I am Thy child - a child of light
A child of the Most High
A child of perfection

As I am
I remind myself that all is well
For all is in Thine All-Knowing-Hands
And Thine All-Guiding-Charge
And above all...
Thine All-Saving-Grace

As I am,
I pray that I never forget
Thy Presence, Thy Protection
Thine All-Solacing-Love
Thine eternal embrace

As I am
I pray that no event or action on my part
Good or evil
Ever avert mine eyes from Thee - Thou God
Who art Creator of ALL

As I am
I pray that I may learn
To love Thee more
To desire Thee more
To seek Thee more
To serve

To live unencumbered
In the thought of Thee alone
To cherish every moment
As a moment of Thine eternal Presence

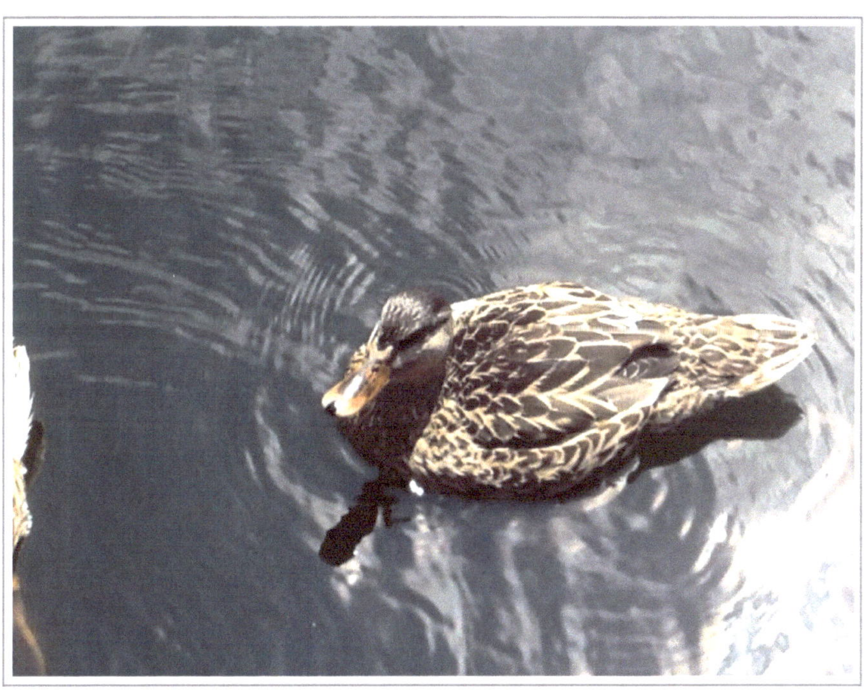

UNCONDITIONAL LOVE

Where there is no fear
Where there is absolute trust
Where there is no need
But the awareness
That all needs will be fulfilled
At the right time

Where there is no judgment
Where there is no self-judgement
Where there is absolute hope
That all is well
And all will ever be well

Where there is perfect stillness
Where there is perfect peace
Where no desire dare tread
Because all desires lie fulfilled

Where there is no loneliness or lack

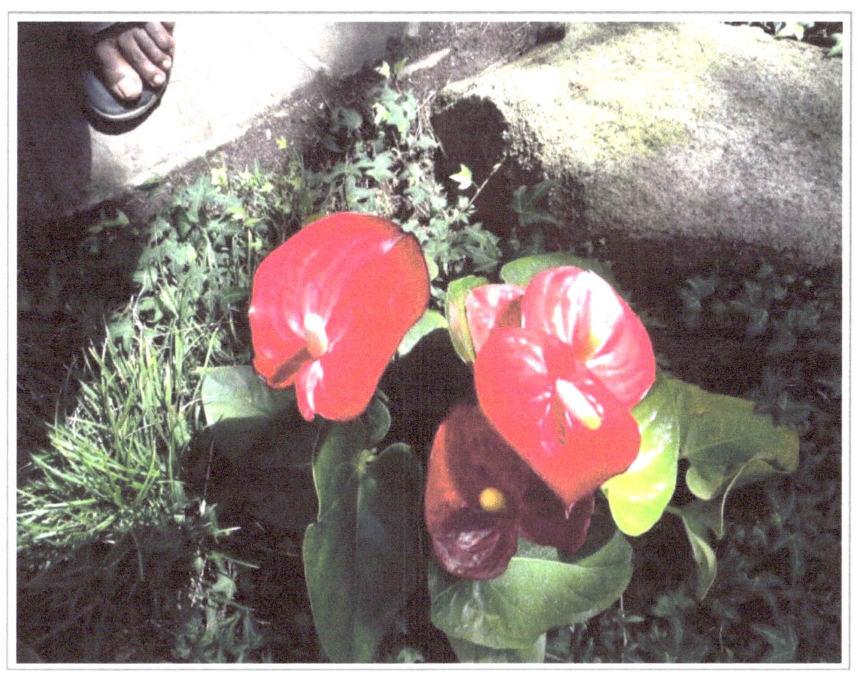

IF ONLY THE WORLD REALLY KNEW

If only the world really knew
With what power God did imbue
The mother....
Who wouldst love when all abandon
Who wouldst give without selfishness
Who wouldst watch with tender care
And always be ready to be there
When most needed

If only the world really knew
With what strength God did imbue
The mother...
Who wouldst gently teach lessons to be learned
Who wouldst give praise even when not earned
Who wouldst relentlessly guard by night and day
Year after year even to a ripe old age

If only the world really knew
Dear God that it is a spark of You
That resides in every mother's breast
That loves with true love that never rests
That protects, that guides, that gives it all
That keeps strong and even if we fall
That catches us and holds us close
Until we know it is Thou
Who art close

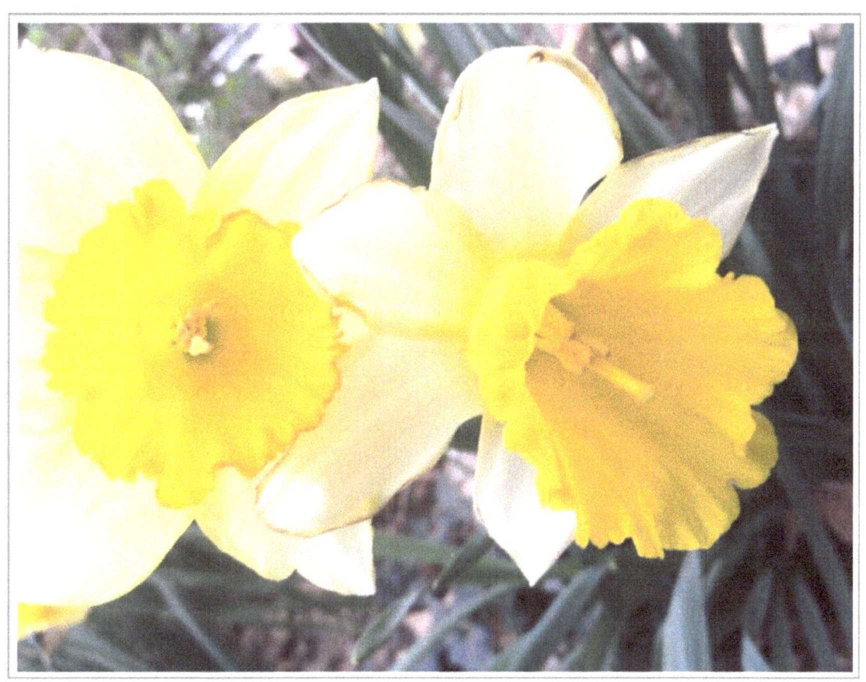

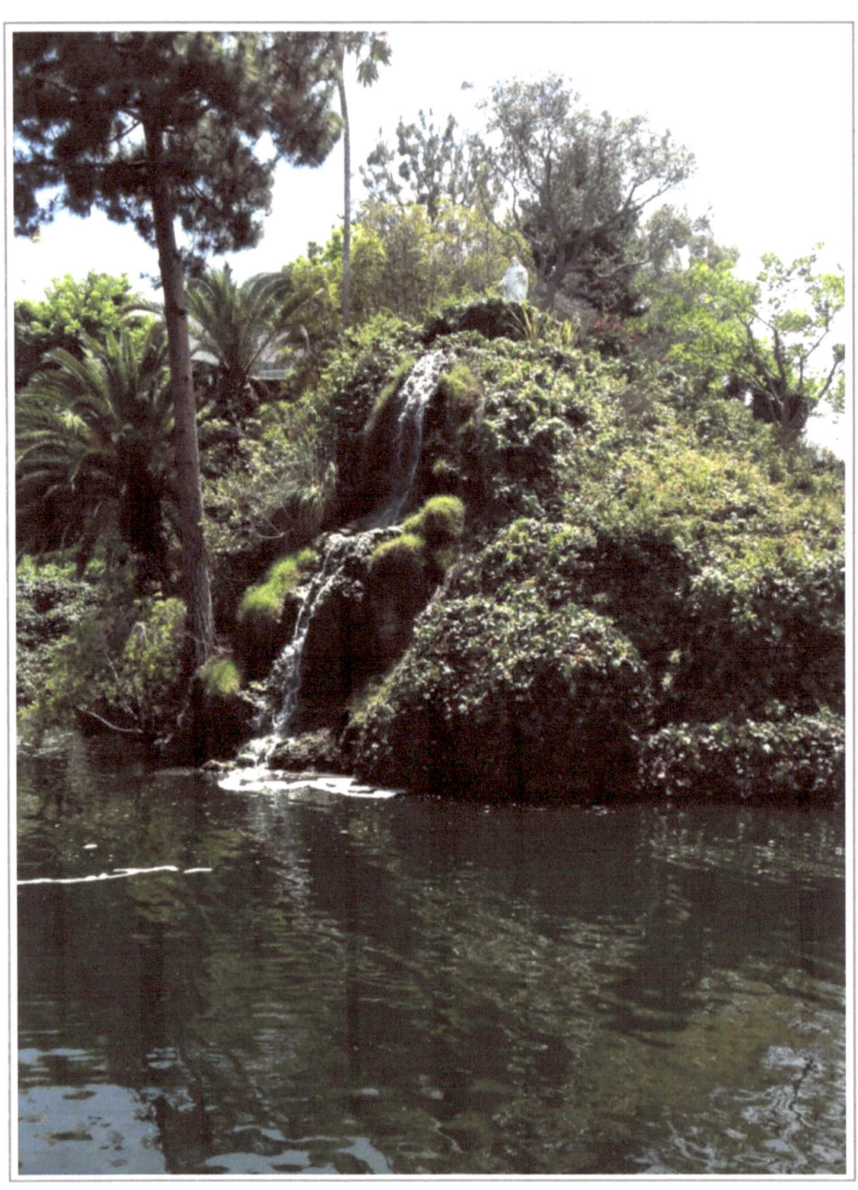

IT IS TIME

Silence come and steal over me
Make me quiet, more quiet again
Open my eyes so that I may see
The trick of restlessness my enemy-friend

Oh mind center yourself
Focus calmly be silent too
Quiet down for perfection of health
Be not disturbed by this mad, mad zoo

Humility as a gushing waterfall
Flow over me and soak me through
Oh precious gem I hear Thy call
And the mind does what it knows it must do

MAYA

Oh dream of life
You dance before these eyes
Unstintingly swaying your hips of delusion
Seemingly, ceaselessly back and forth

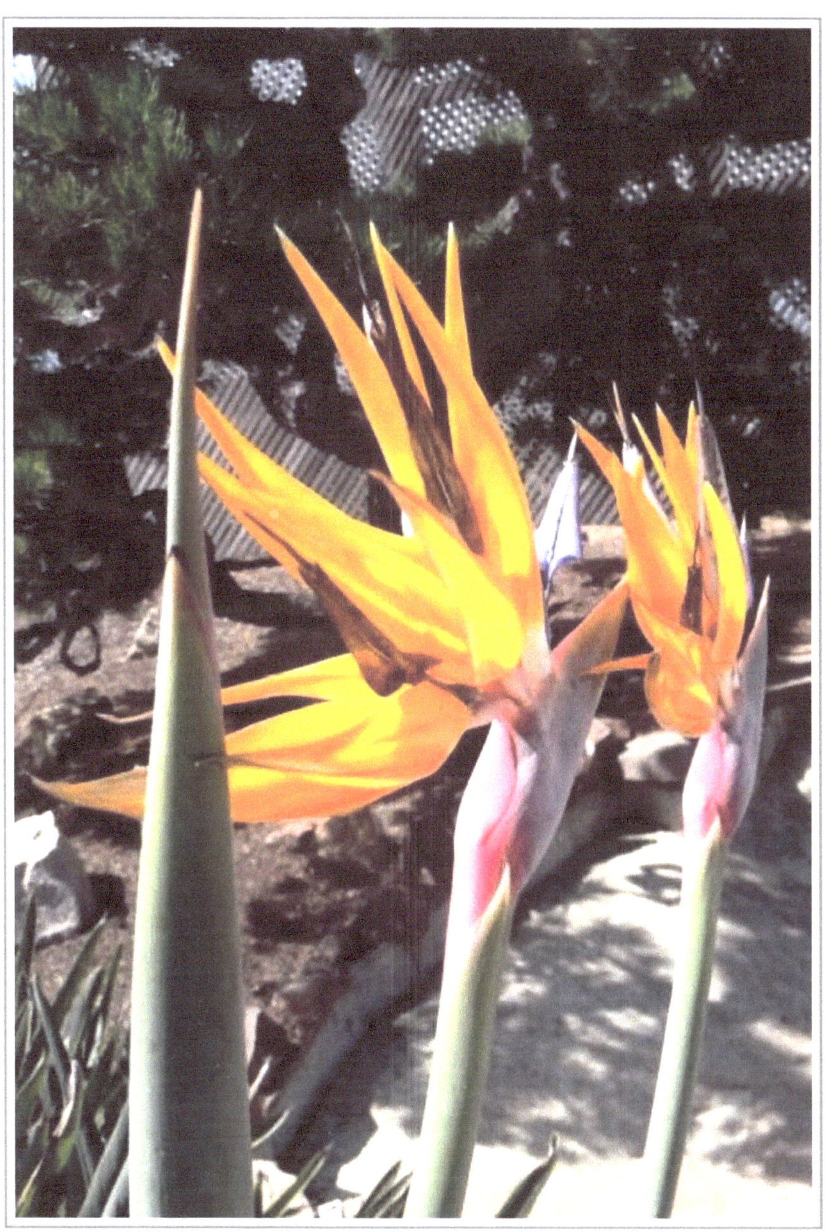

NEW RESOLVE

This futile path
Upon which I trod
Must be deserted
With its useless clod
A greater way
Must be embarked upon
A way that leads
Into the dawn
Of self awareness
God bless me

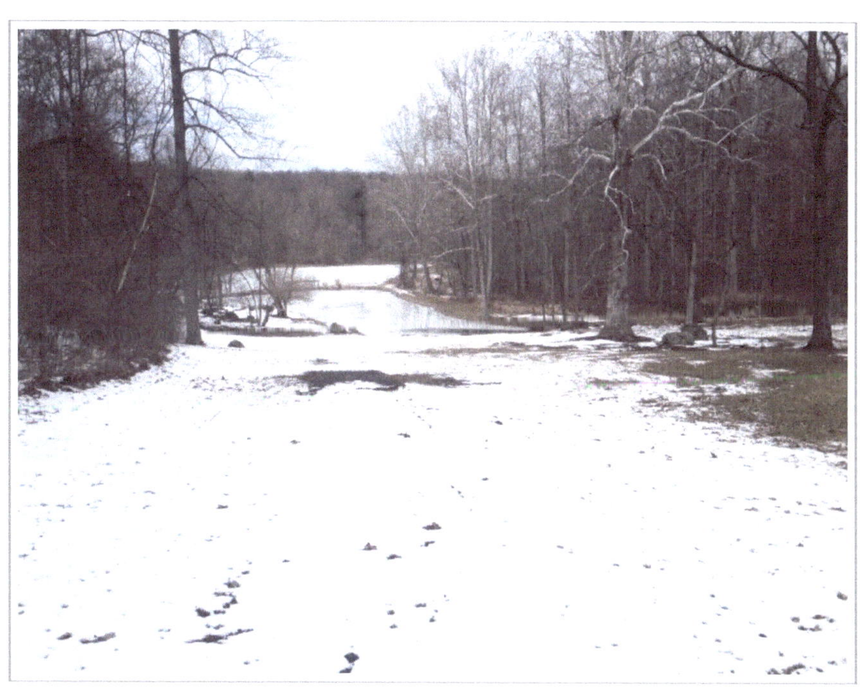

HER

Ball of fire
Glow so bright
From whence, from where
Comes this heavenly light
God's empire
There, there and there
Uncircumscribed for eternity

Always to be
The light of God shining
So kind so compassionate
I cry, cry, cry
Signing my soul's love unto
Her
So great.

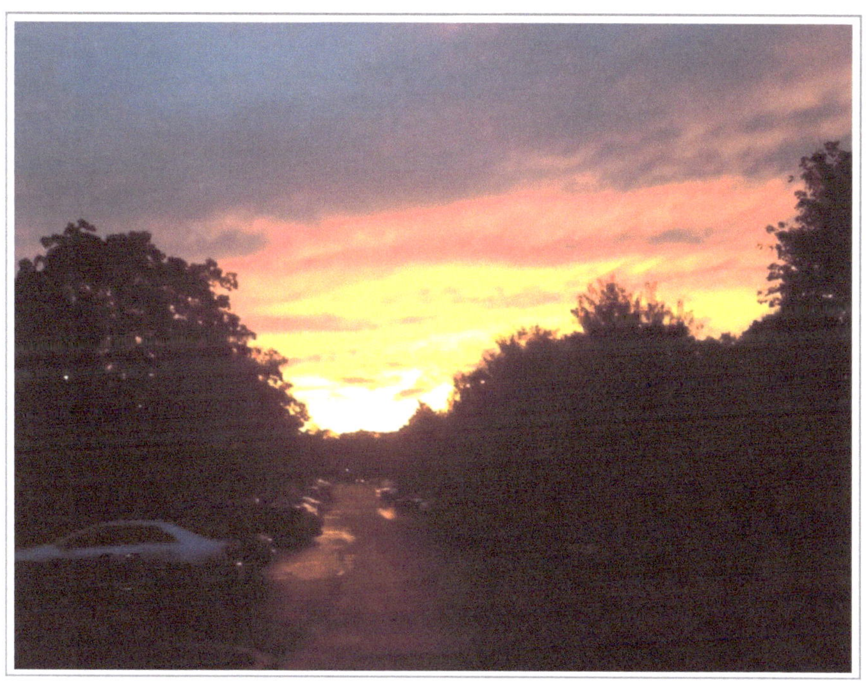

GOD

Ocean of love roaring
Sweet as doves soaring
Heavenly bells ringing
Child's voice singing
Heart yields song
Vibrating for long
Peace flows over
Never grows older
Eyes see light
Dreams take flight

Separate no more
No delusions' war
All one is
Unity all is
Harmony forever
Disloyalty never
No roam after roam
God alone
God alone

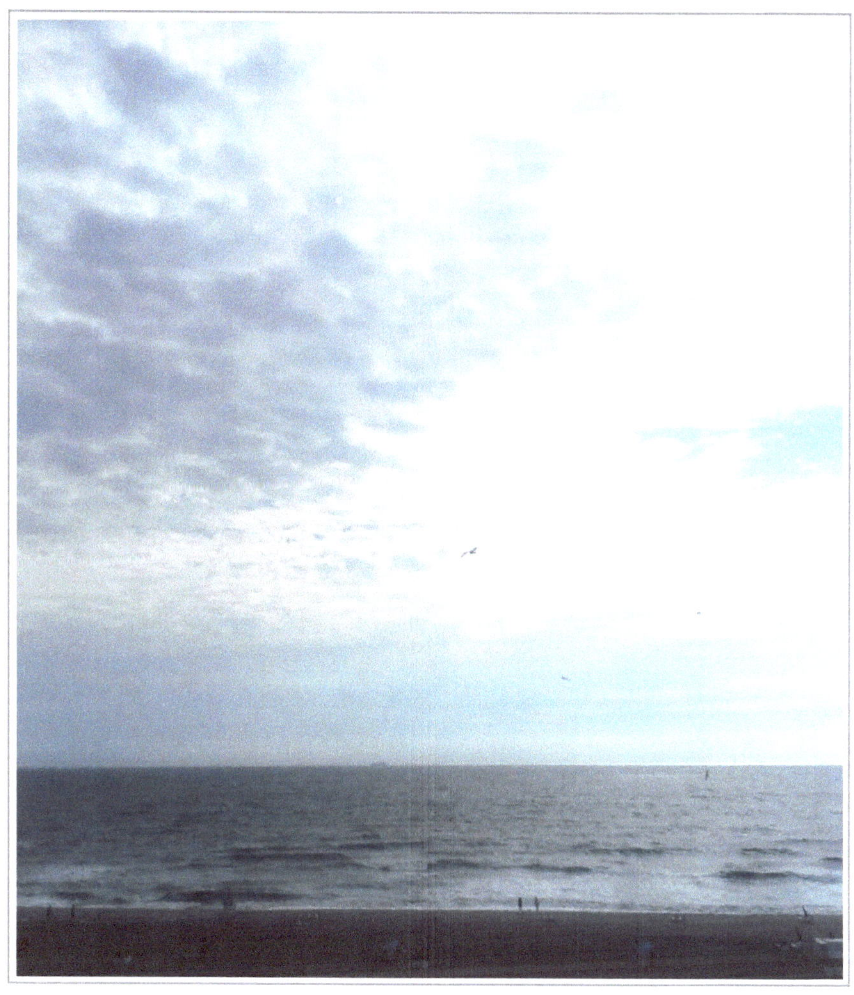

SILENCE

the brother of peace
the wise one chooses this way
because in silence one can listen,
by listening one can hear
by hearing one can merge and know what truth is
silence goes beyond the simple shutting of the mouth for
even then, when the mouth is quiet and vibrations of words
are subdued from manifestation,
still the thoughts and desires sing their songs
(they don't want to be silent they want to be heard
they want the world to constantly know they exist)
ah but by concentration's power they must be silenced
by the mind's power they must be stilled
for only then can what is real,
what is humble
what is true
be shown

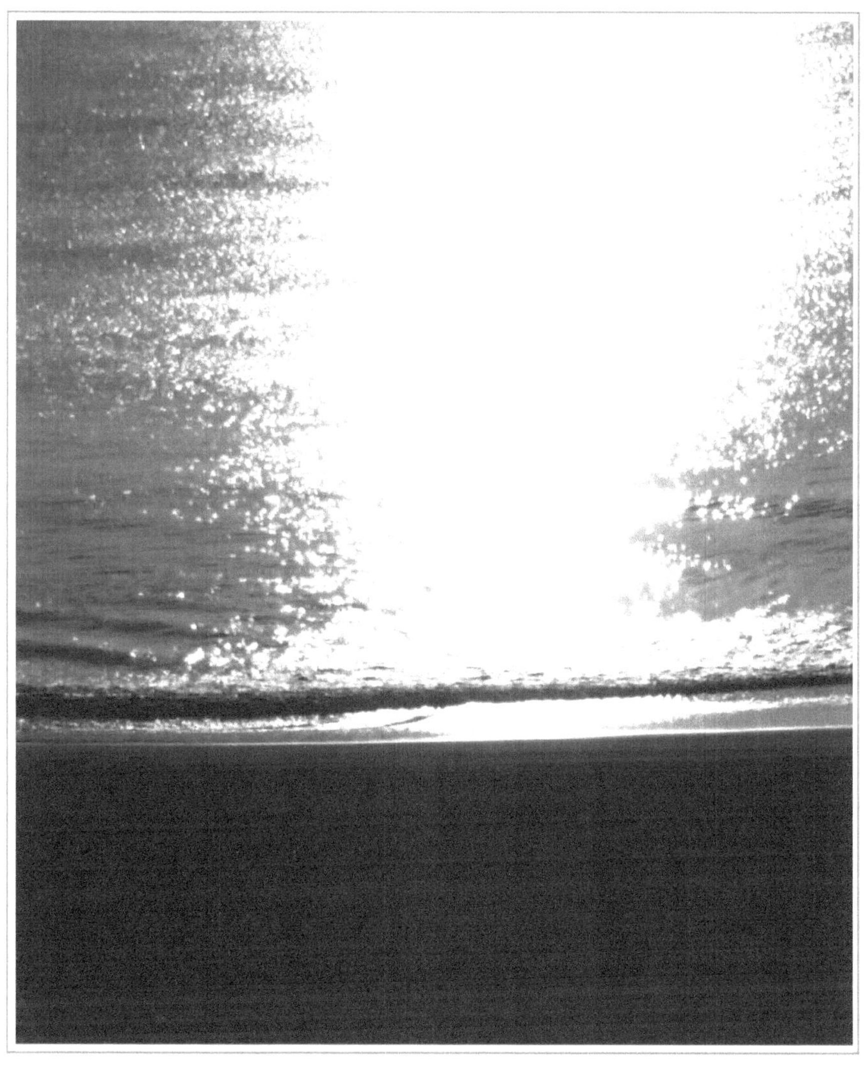

MY SECRET PAL

Oh my secret pal
Who hides so well
That I often forget
That Thou art there

Oh my secret pal
Who hides so well
That I often don't know
That Thou art there

Oh my secret pal
Who hides so well
That I often find it hard
To contact Thee

DEATH

Death stares at me
From every corner
Every angle
Everywhere

Death looms up
Before my seemingly
Helpless self
Promising to one day
Meet me
And whisk me off
Into the unknown

Death, what are you?
Who are you?
And why do you
Look at me so

Is it to prod me?
To push me?
To make me wonder?
To make me look?
To make me seek to
Understand?

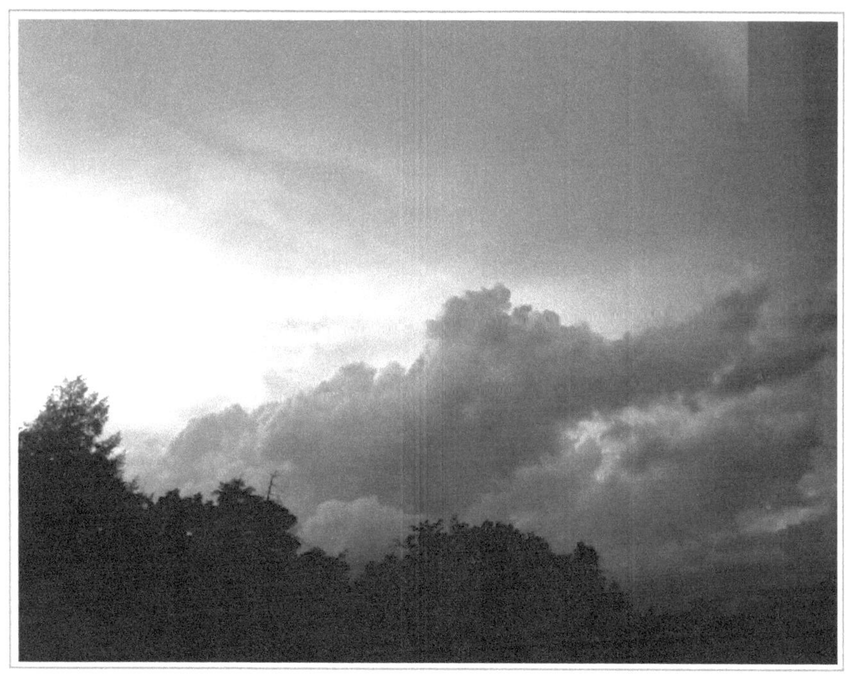

LOVE

My heart is like a well
Waiting to be filled

My heart is like a river
Ready to spread life giving water

My heart is like a speck
So tiny, so unsure of what's next

My heart is like an ocean
So large, so overwhelming

My heart hungers for one thing

Love...

Love fills the well
Love gives life
Love protects the unsure
Love is abundant within itself
Love is the food to satisfy
The hungering heart.

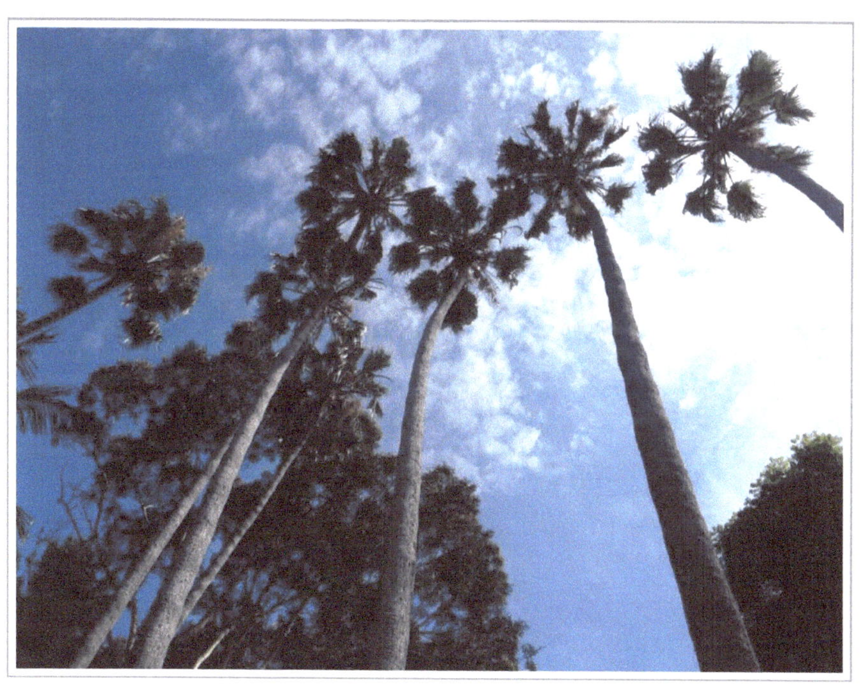

I AM YOURS

Silent whisper on the
Gentle breeze
Say it clearly my heart
You must appease
The thrill and impassioned
Sense I feel
Engulfs my whole being
Is it real
Soar in the skies a light
Chase all the darkness
Make things bright
My heart is Yours
For life

Waiting yearning, no more
Now fulfilled
Endless satisfaction mounting
Joy never killed
Passionate glory thrill after thrill
Embrace my being
There's no until
Dazzle my heart with Your Mysterious glow
Carry me through eternity
On Your ceaseless flow

THE THOUGHT OF YOU

The thought of You is all I need

To get me through the day

The thought of You is all I need

To wipe my tears away

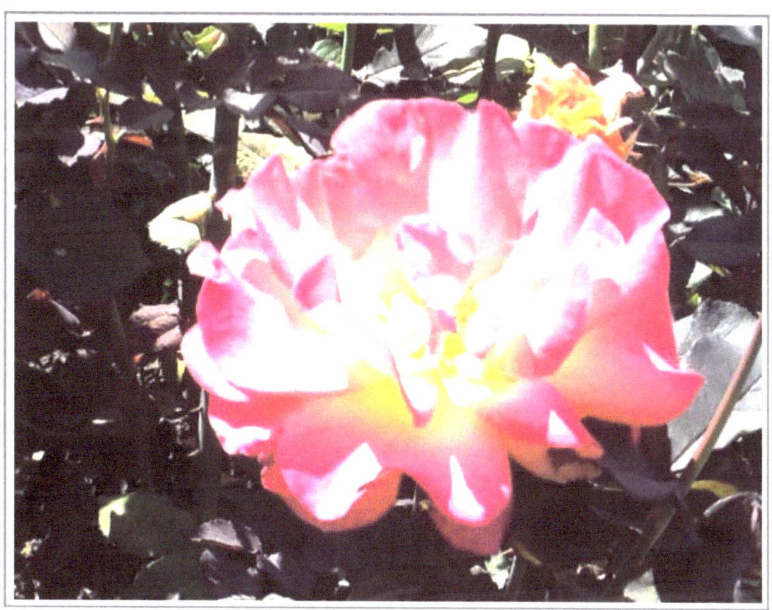

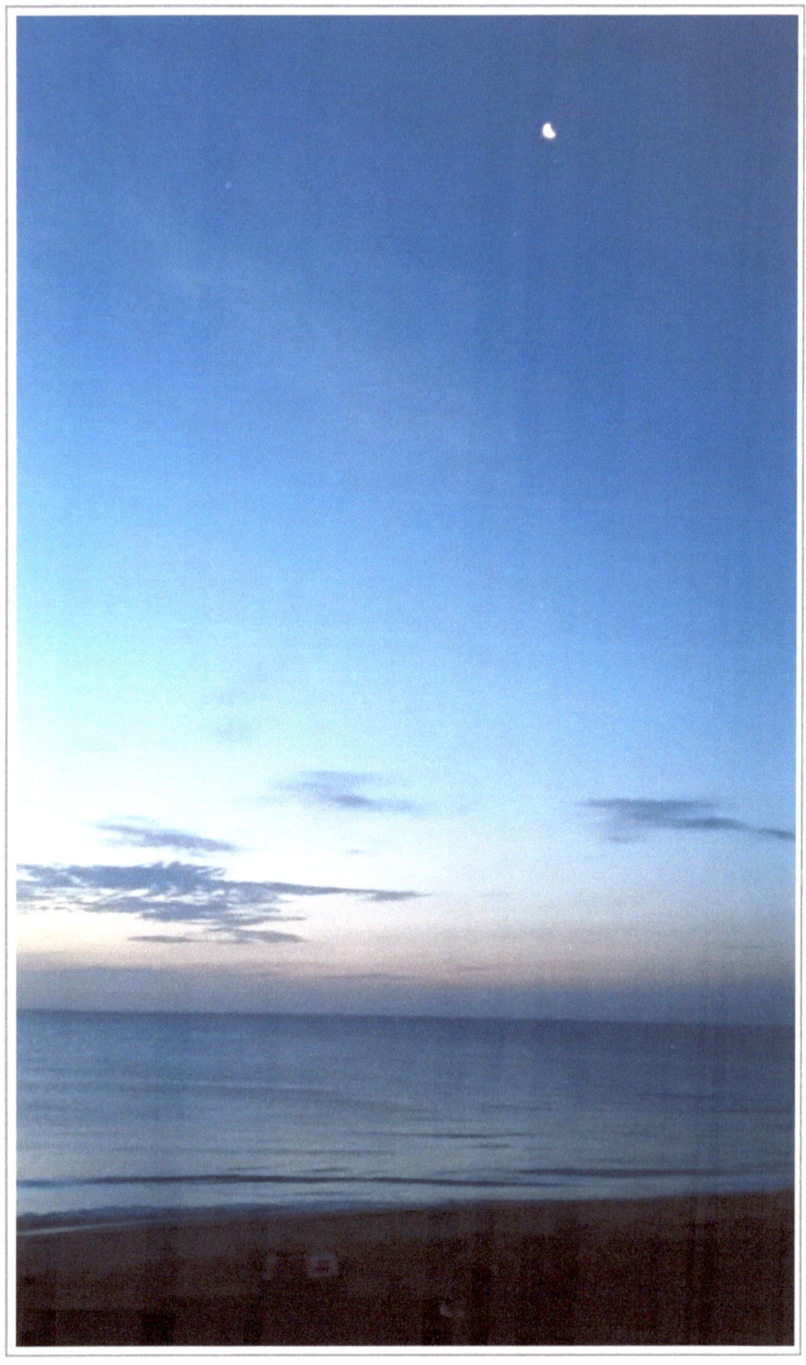

DEEPER

Fear not, forge ahead

Penetrate the darkness

Sit still

Very still

Move not a muscle

Nor a thought

In the depth of depths

Find greater depth

Deeper, deeper, deeper

NECTAR

My heart is seeking

To be filled

With the nectar of love

To be thrilled

Day after day

Until all sadness

Is driven away

Oh Sweet Nectar

Where hidest Thou

Here is Thy thirsty

Child, seeking, searching, looking

Come, oh Sweet Mystery of Youth, come

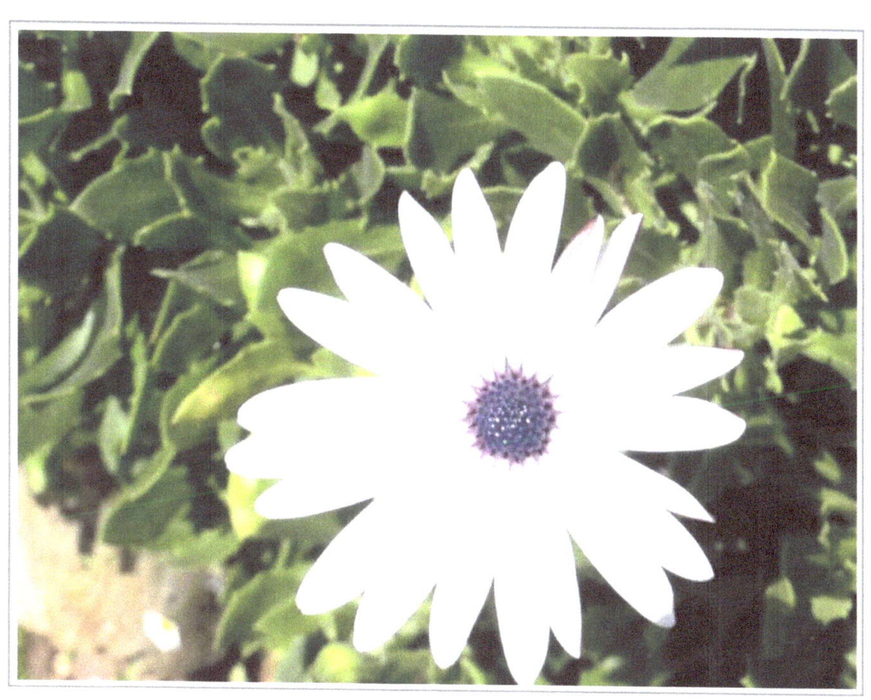

MASTER

Master of mine

Oh great one divine

Show me the way

The best thou didst follow

Give me thy magic

Strength to go on

And on with thee

In the night with thee

Dawn by dawn

Let time dreams

Life lose all meaning

Let the great goal

Be my only sight

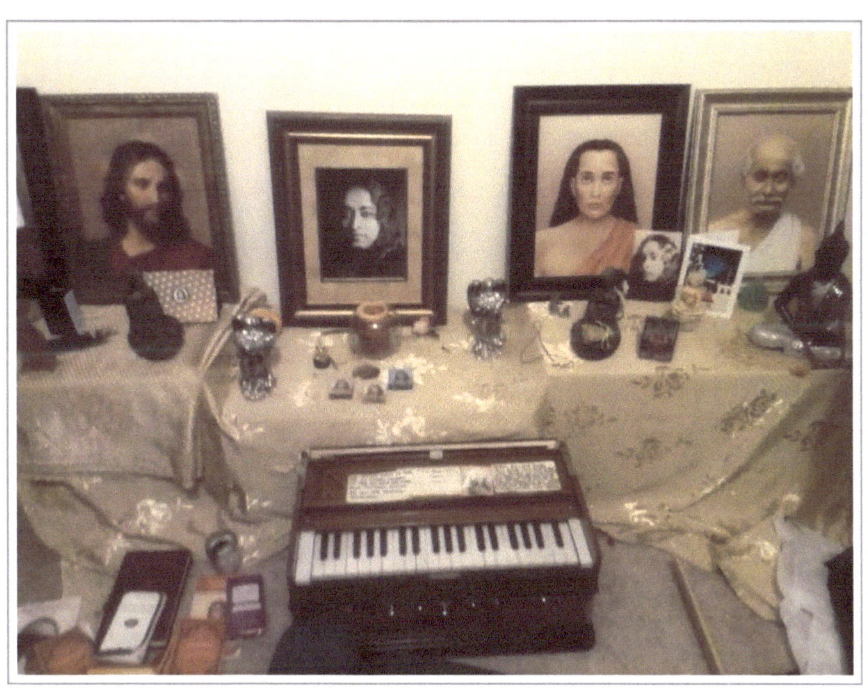

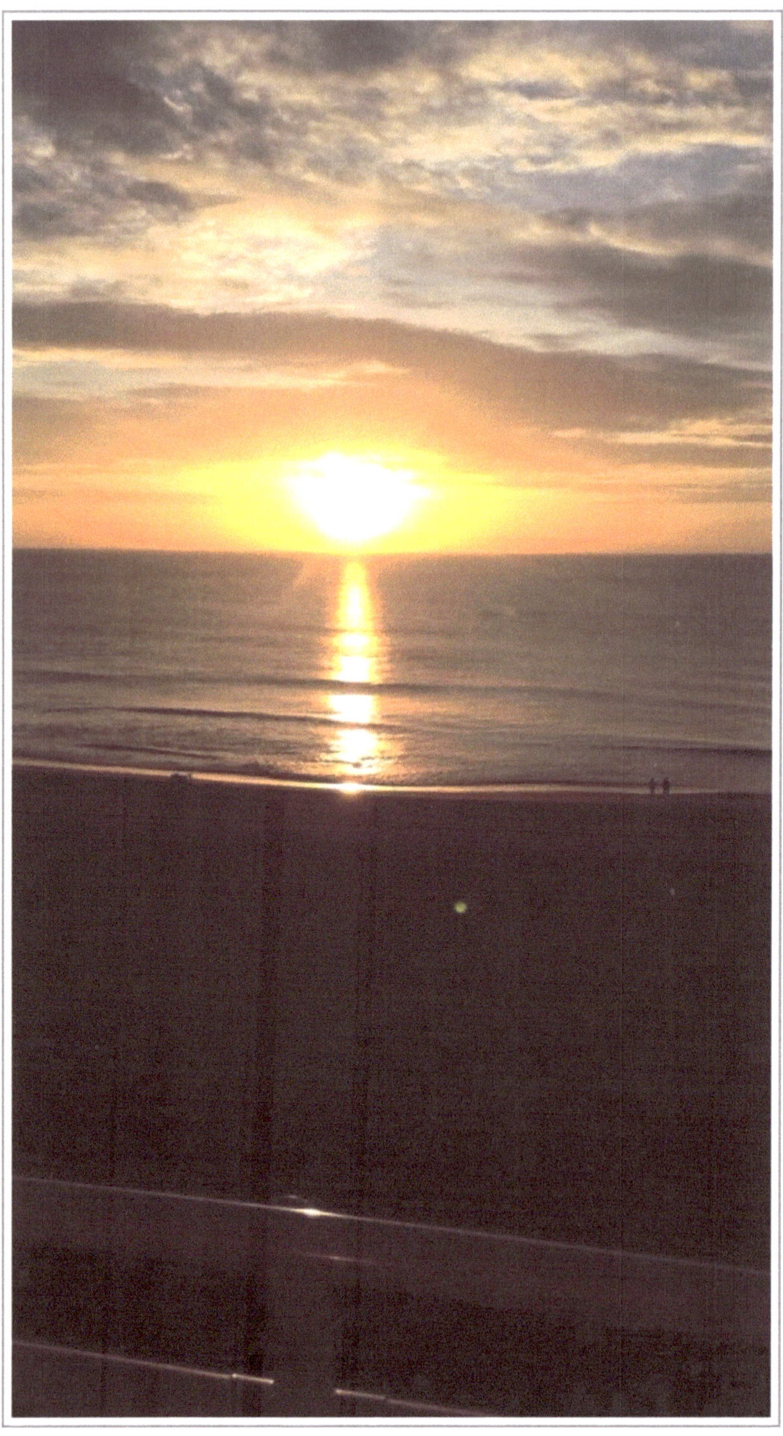

NOT REAL

Dare you tell me

That all this is real

When the truth

Through the great ones

Is self-revealed

When the method

By which truth can be conceived

Lies plain before you

No more be you deceived

When the power in your hands

Is vaster than all the lands

When by wish and by will alone

Soil you can till

When earth no longer binds you

By gravity's pull

When facet eludes not you

For all perceptive is your eye

CHAINS

Bound by many chains

I seem to be

But, verily, what chains

Can bind me?

When infinite power and force

Exists within

Alas I believe it is I

I have chained myself

Unbeknownst to myself

Each link, each binding cord

I have, myself, created

Fashioned by power in me

And this very same power

Will set me free!

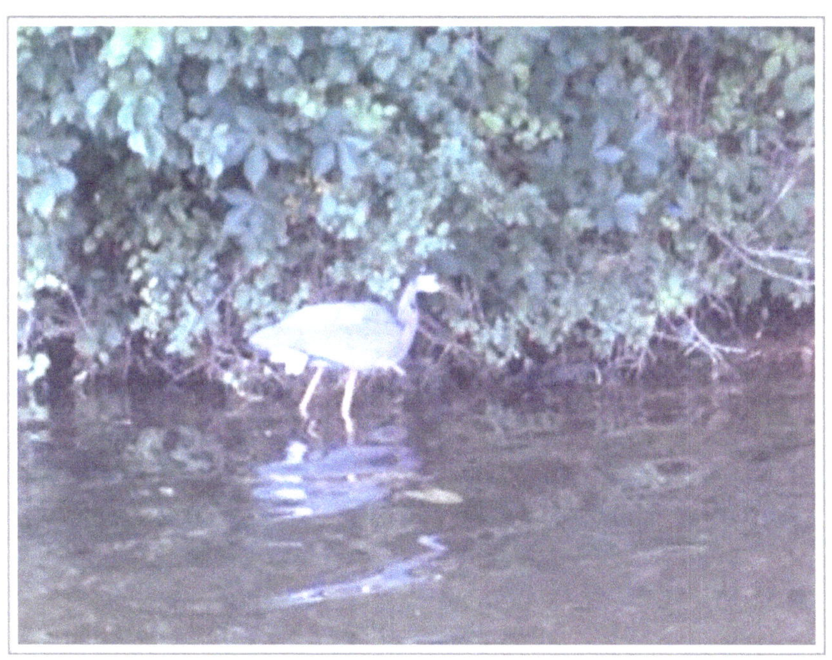

PATIENT

I am as patient as the mother
Who graciously watches over her child
As he grows, as he falls,
As he picks himself up.

I am as patient as the lover
Who awaits his reunion with his
Long distant love as she works to
Complete whatever task she must complete
Before their meeting

I am as patient as the rock,
Still, almost motionless, who awaits the time
Of transformation to some higher life form
Who watches the seconds as they slip into
Minutes as they slip into hours, days, years
Human lifetimes

I am as patient as the tree;
The redwood who sees years come and go
And stands there quietly, peacefully,
Exuding wisdom unknown unfathomable
The mystery of life.

I am as patient as the stigmatist
Heroically bearing unbearable pain again and again
Without complaint, without resentment
With hardly a sigh
To express the anguish of suffering.

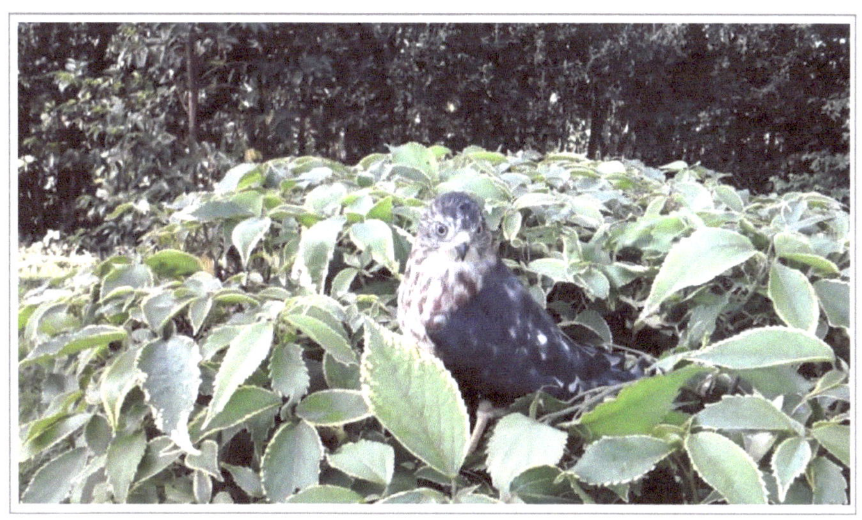

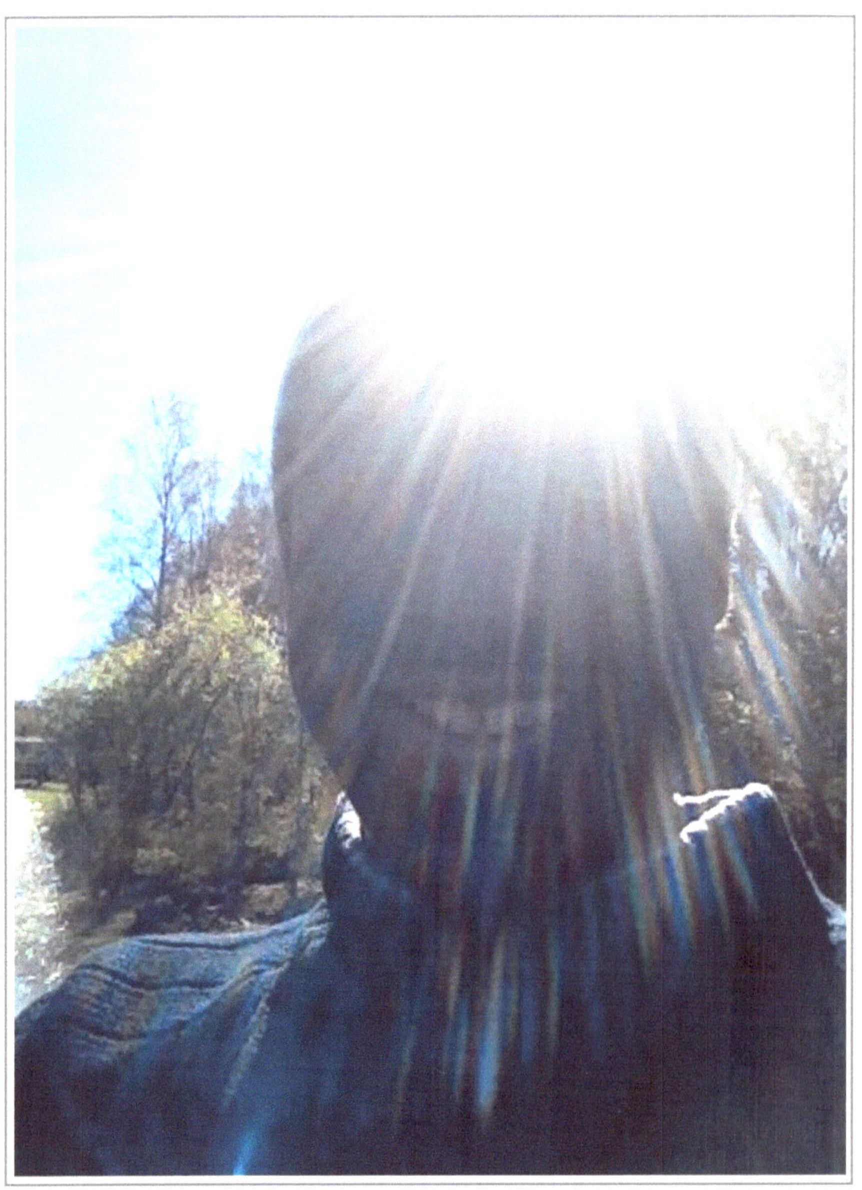

I REACH FOR THINE EMBRACE

Lost in this dark forest of life
I groped around in the darkness
Trying to find my way
Trying to glimpse the light of day

When my desire crystallized strong
I knew it wouldn't be long
A beam of light came shining through
A beacon that would lead me back to you

I followed this dream as best I could
You guided me as I knew you would
Many a time I did go astray
You always brought me back to that sacred ray

And now the beam a little brighter grows
And my heart gets excited because my soul knows
Not much longer do I have to wait,
To see the full and brilliant light of day

And when at last from darkness I emerge
With uncontrolled passion and unrestrained urge
I will fling my self, my heart my love
Fully into Thine eternal embrace

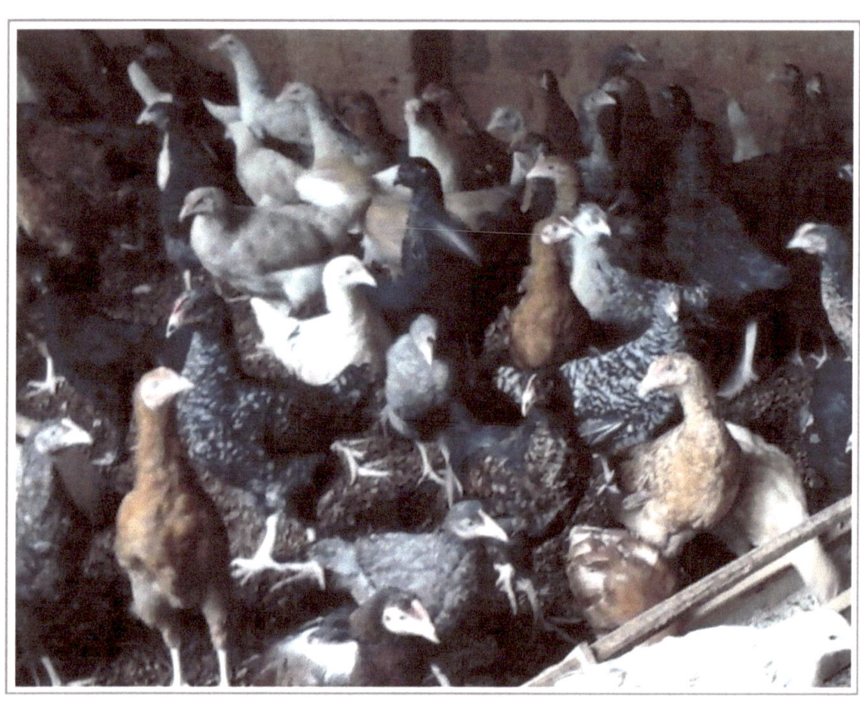

FREE FROM THE CHICKEN COOP

In the dark of silent night,
I pray to Thee who art so bright
I pray that Thou into my temple come
And make me and Thee again as one

For many years my soul has roamed
And now I yearn to come back home
I yearn for peace, I yearn for bliss
I yearn for Thy touch and magic kiss

So leave me not in this dark placc
Release my soul that I feel Thine embrace
Take me to a higher place
Remove the fear the shame and disgrace

At last I must see the brilliant love
That guides and protects and descends like a dove
From heaven to earth in a beautiful swoop
Saving this child from the chicken coop!

FREEDOM'S FLIGHT

My mind is made up and with fiery will
I seek Thy bliss thrill upon thrill
I break chains and chords
That me do tie
And whisk myself home
Way up high
I soar above boundaries
That seek me to bind
Into infinite space
Thy face to find
With telescopic speed
And unbridled pace
I zoom unfailingly
Completing the race
At last in Thine arms
I find me rest
And release myself to Thee
Whom I love best

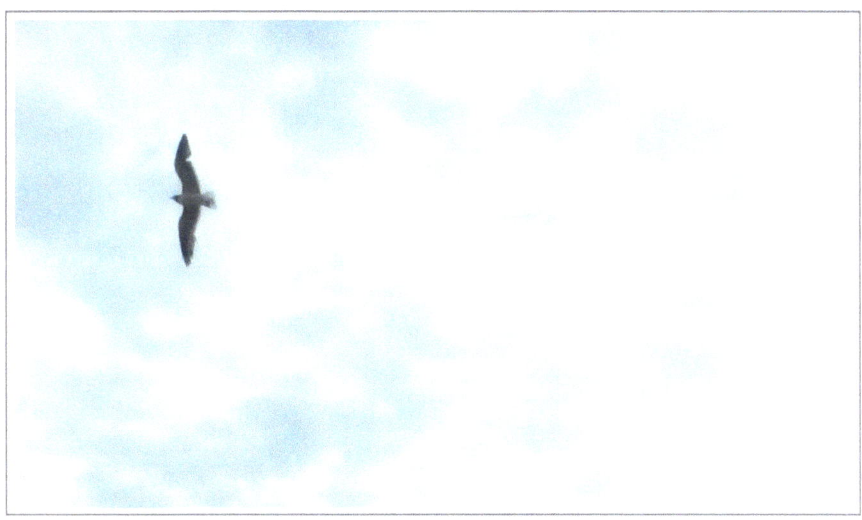

IS IT SO HARD

Is it so hard to love
When we know we want love?

Is it so hard to wish the best
For those who cross our path
When we know we want the best for ourselves

Is it so hard to share what we have
When we know if we were destitute
We would want others to share with us

Is it so hard to think and act for God
When we know God loves us unconditionally
When we know God is with us constantly
When we know that God feeds us
When we know that God gives us breath
When we know that God digests our food
When we know God is here, now, constantly
And unconditionally loving us
From moment to moment?

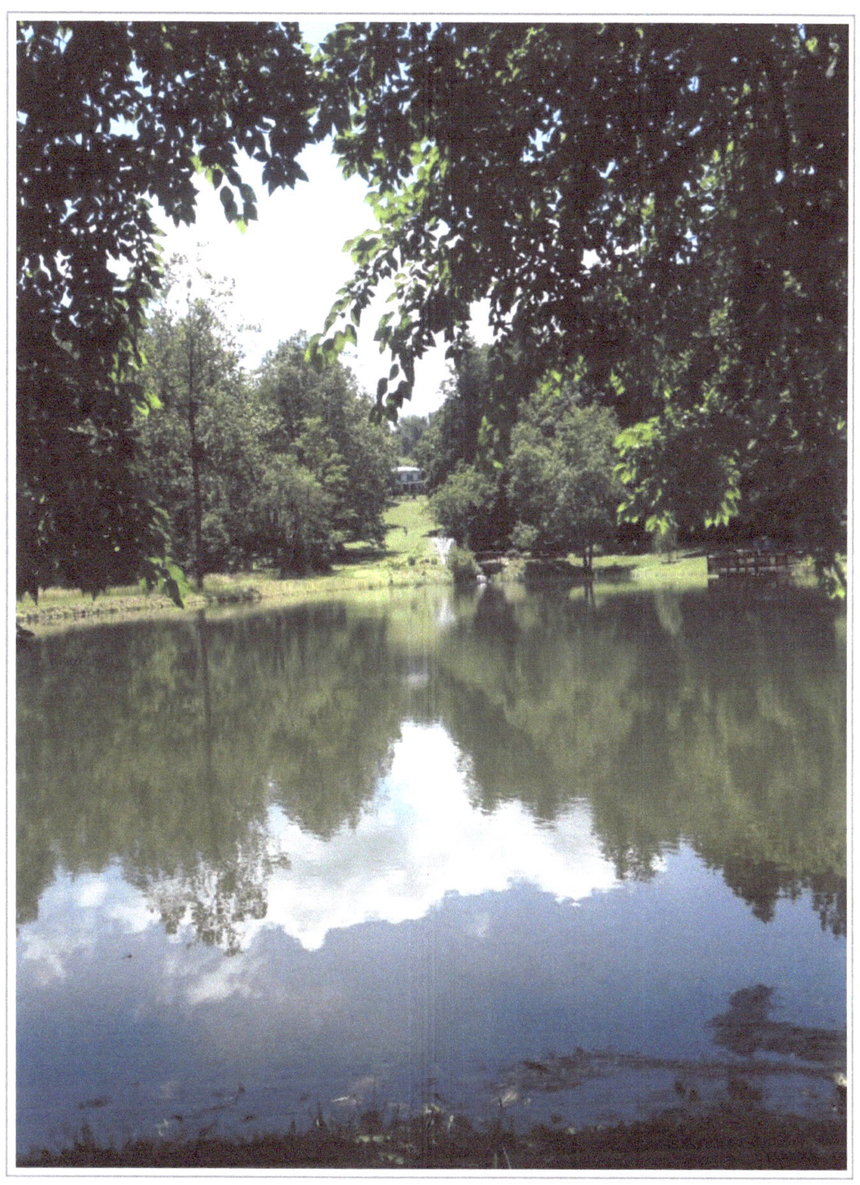

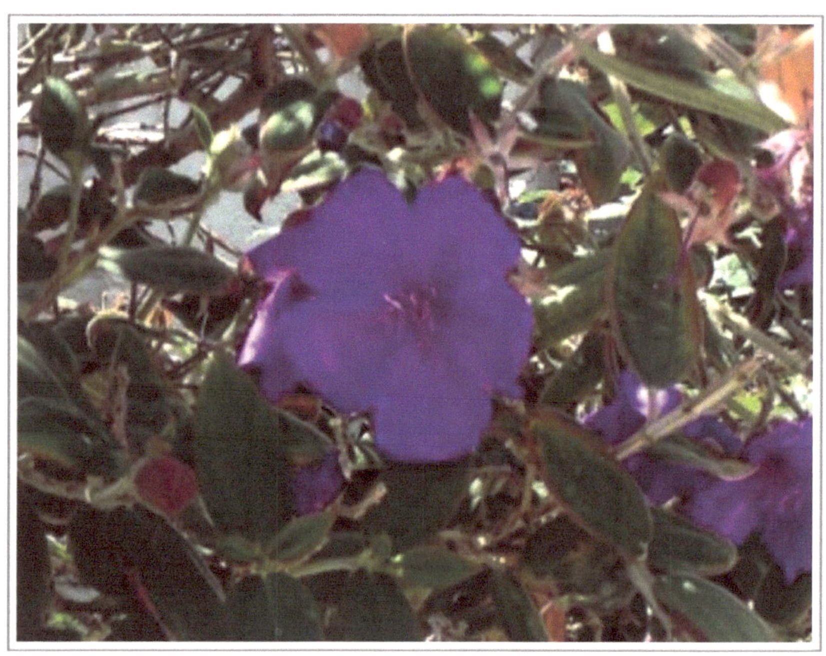

MY GRATITUDE

Don't thank me
Because I am lazy
My motivation is of
My God above
All that I do
Is inspired by Him
He is true
He makes me win
So when I seem good
Or to do much
Remember, you should
That it is God's touch
I turn your thanks
Over to His hands
He owns all banks
I am His great fan
Indeed Who is doer of all
Who catches each one of us
Who breaks our fall
So turn your heart
With grateful love
To the great God within
In Heaven, below and above

FAITH

I look at what's happening in my life
I rebel because I don't understand
I do not see the big picture
I see the injustice that happens to me
Yet I know that I am not fully clear of responsibility
But art Thou not my protector?
Then there must be good or at least a lesson in the event
I know that I have responsibility for what happens to me
I create my life constantly by my thoughts and actions
I know also that I cling to old forms to habits born of fear
I cling to that which I think will undo my loneliness
I cling to old dirt, when I know at least, intellectually that
All I need is Thee
It seems so hard to give up the little things
And hold on to Thee alone
Yet at some point that is what I must do
Must I suffer through countless humiliations before I wise up?
Must I torture my body, mind and heart
Before I decide to look to Thee alone?
I know I am impatient and I need to be fulfilled now
I tire of this earthly drama with its ups and downs
But when will I change?
I want to change but I am afraid, I am lost
I have no support from people in this world
I only have support from Thee.
So why not turn to Thee, who alone, cares for me, knows me,
Knows my needs, feels for me, loves me unconditionally?

SO SIMPLE

The nature of life
Is so simple you know
All this strife
And seeming lack of flow

The word from thought
Produced by will
Removes distraught
And negativity kills.
The thought creates
And has made all
Our speech orates
Making gerent or thrall

So reclaim your omnipotence
Cease the infantile wails
Kill all indifference
Let your essence prevail

Climb the ladder of remembrance
Rung by rung
Seek help from the Agents
Let your life not be unsung
(A sense of self is necessary)

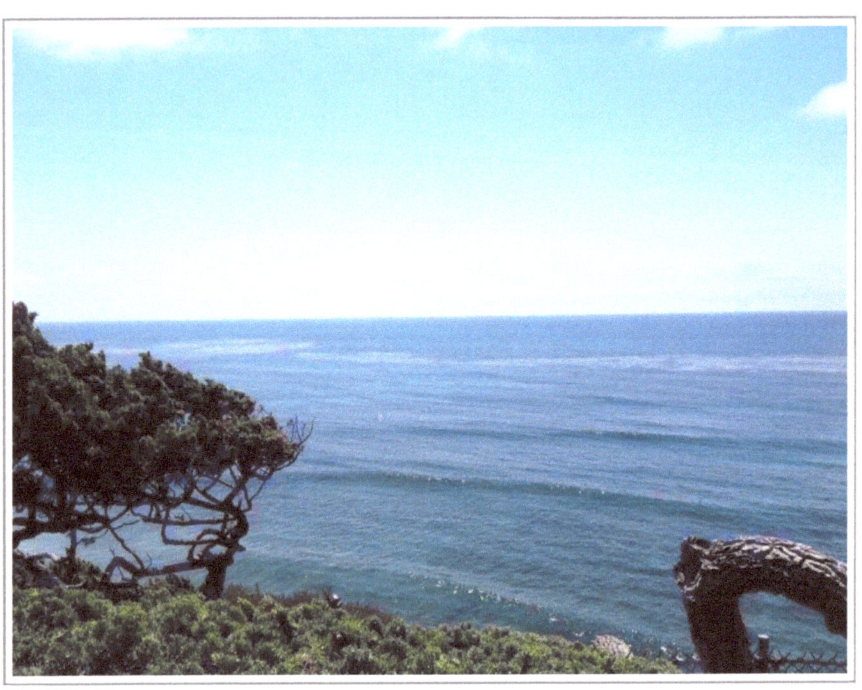

MY ONLY LOVE

You are my one
And only love
Though many hearts
Flock to You as doves
Do to a park
Full of nurturing seeds
My heart bleeds
For You.

I want to feel
That love from head to heel
In every fiber of my being
Seeing You is my only goal.

THE MYSTERY OF LIFE

Why is it that there is a world out there
And a world in here
So far
Yet so near
The stars
Float in endless space
And atoms dance in inner space
Laced with energies
Designed with grace
My mind is a probe
Looking searching, seeking, diving, dipping
To understand what's going on
So strong
Is my desire to know
The meaning of the flow...
To penetrate the depths of reality
I seize every opportunity that promises an answer
I want to be free!

I move forward but hardly recognize it
Because my progress is always bit by bit
I want big moves
Leaps beyond boundaries
I want to tear myself from gravity
I yearn to have the answers here and now
Not to ponder the world or wonder how
It all came to be
Or be lost in the thought of me
Free is what I want to be. Free

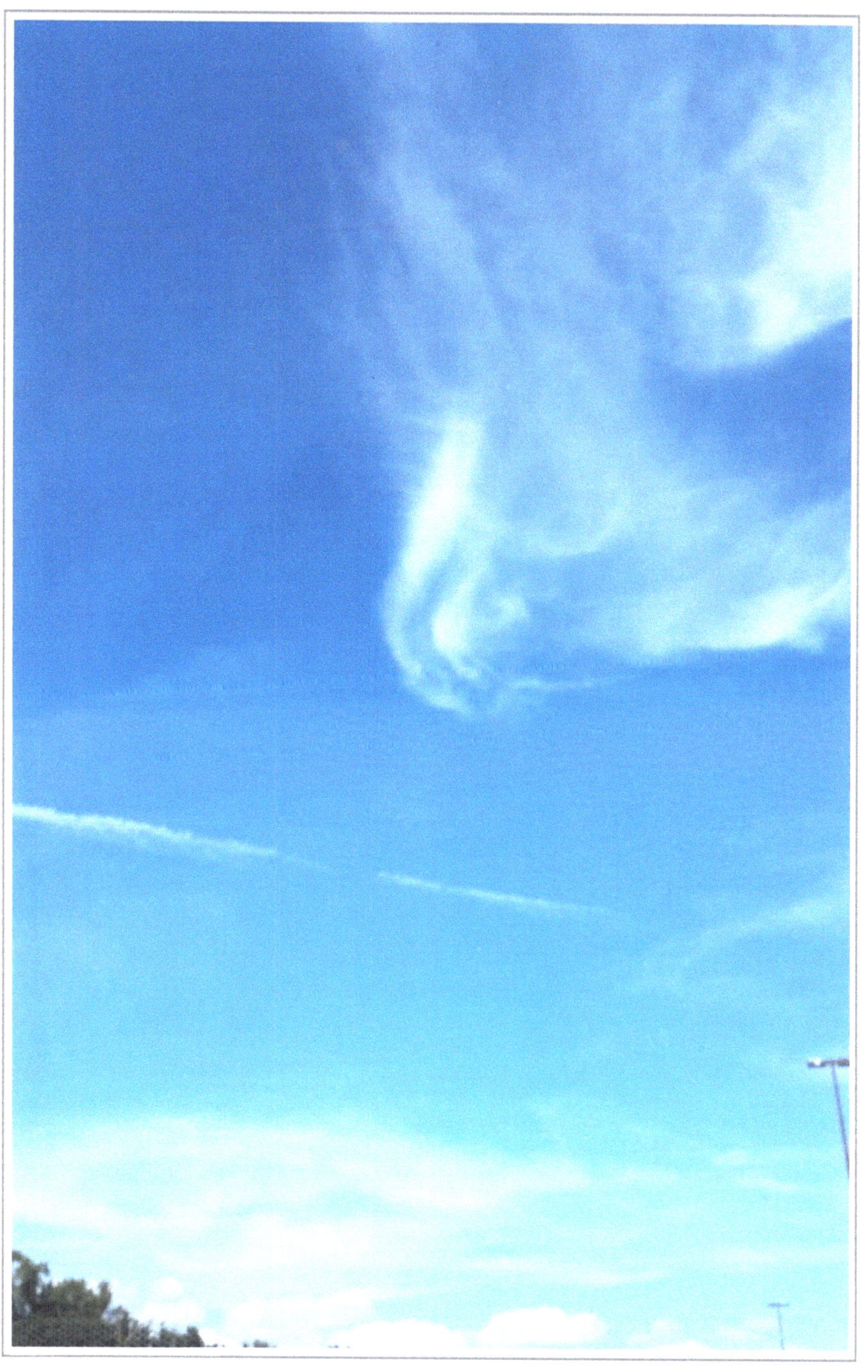

INFINITY

I believed them
When they said I could't fly
I believed them
Why would they lie?
I believed them
When they said I wasn't smart
When they covered my soul
And pierced my heart
With doubt and fear
Year after year
I became more and more
Caged in, by the iron bars of my own imagination
Dull from lack of concentration
Sick from hopelessness
Diseased by seeming helplessness

But all was not lost forever
Because I found the path
Back to my infinite treasure
The source of it all
My wings to fly
My imagination beyond the limit of any sky
Everything I ever was and ever will be
Right here, right here, right here with me.
By the strength of my own mind

I thought I lost my infinity
Infinity cannot be lost
Only imagined gone
Every part of this conundrum
Will sing the song of Freedom

WHAT I FEEL NOW

I feel restless
Like something is about to happen
Or I want something to happen
Like I want excitement or adventure
To be bad

But I don't want to be bad
Because afterward I'll feel sad
That I've been bad
So what is all that about

Why am I struggling against myself for my Self?
How do I win this game
How do I evade the pain
How do I do all this and remain sane?

What to do, the answers aren't plain or clear
Nobody whispers them in my ear
Love yourself is the voice I hear

Just love yourself no matter how bad you think you are
No matter what you do
Remember God is the doer
To Him alone be true
He doesn't judge you for your crazy deeds
He just embraces you and tries to care for your needs

But you can't be with Him if you think He's far
Reach into your forehead for the shining star
The eye that bespeaks His presence
And never, no matter what you do
Let ugly thoughts tie you down like glue

Don't let them in
Reject them one and all
Embrace yourself, embrace God
And you cannot fail.

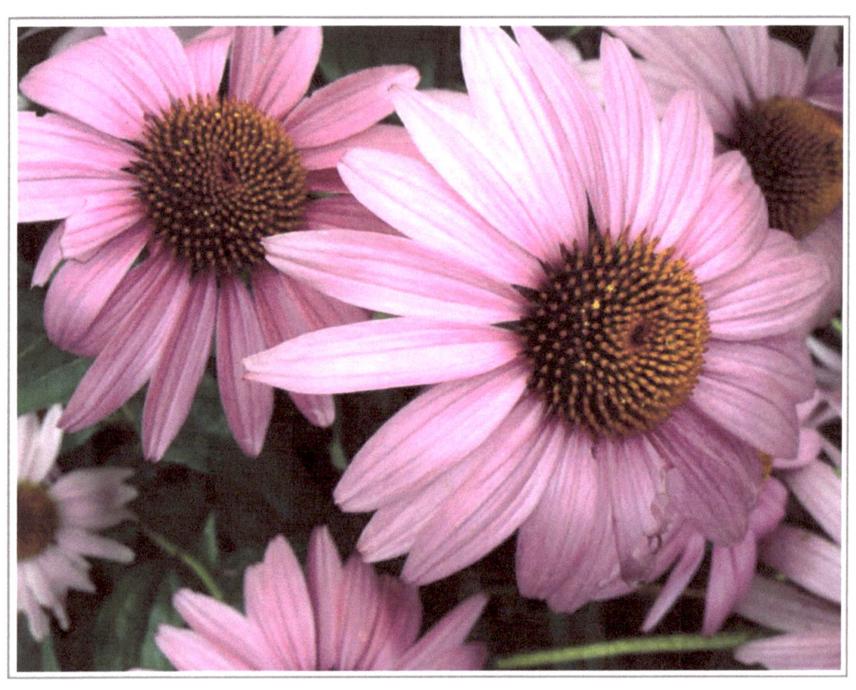

MY DESIRE

All I ever wanted was Your warm embrace
To see the light in Your eyes
When the sun shines on Your face
To feel You close with every breath I take
To know You'll never leave me no matter what's at stake

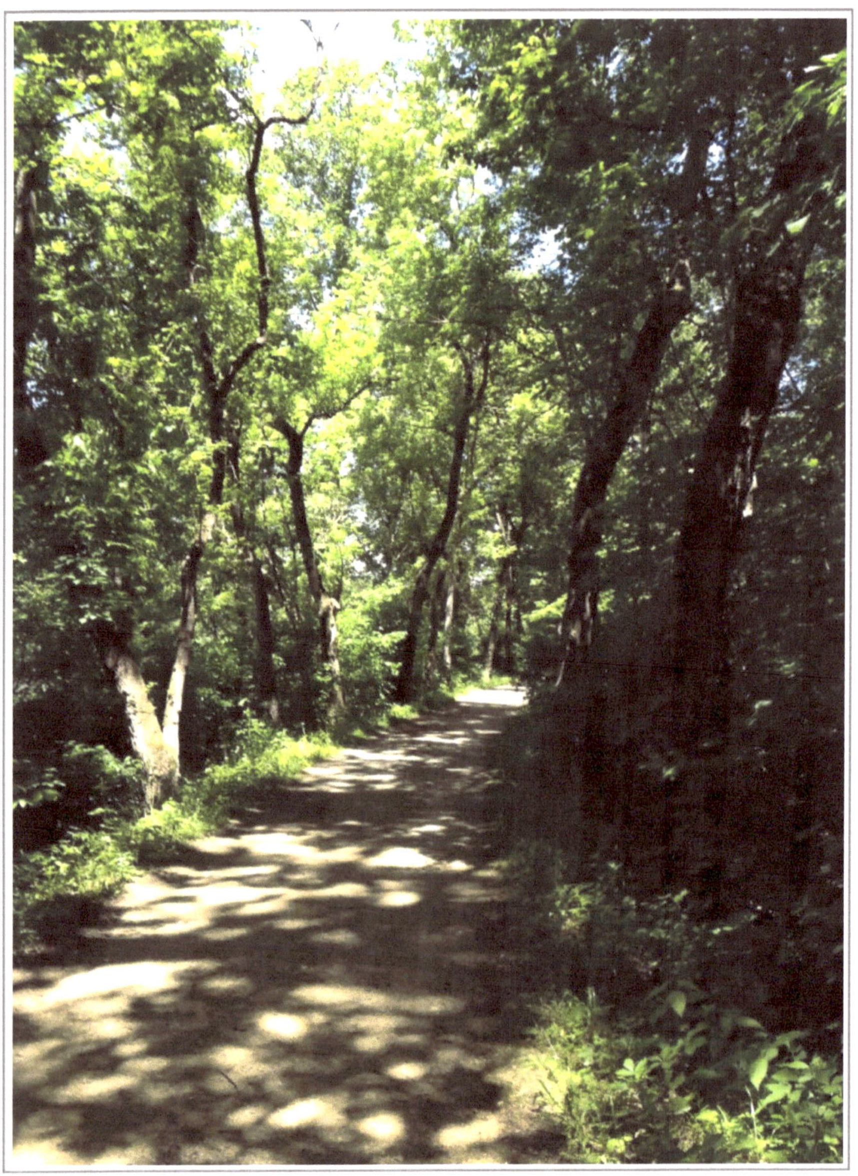

DO I BELIEVE IN YOU

I ask myself why I trod this lonely path
If I really believe in You, am I really lonely?
Are You not with me, always by my side?
Even though hidden to my blind eyes?

If I believe You are love and that You love me
And that I'm Your child
How then, can I feel fear, loneliness, lack
Need, want, desire, and unhappiness?
Does not love nurture, protect, defend,
Embrace, and give happiness?
So what of it?

I believe You, I believe in You
You are my reality
I refuse and reject any thought that You are far away
I refuse and reject my senses that show not Your presence
I disbelieve my lying thoughts that say I am alone

I embrace You, who art eternally with me by my side
Guiding, guarding and protecting me in every moment
Never even an inch away-everyday, every hour, every second,
Every microsecond, every before second
Thou art here; can it be otherwise?
Can it really be otherwise?
No.
So what do I say to my doubting, fearful mind?
How do I remove the blinds?

SET ME FREE

Only You can set me free
I bow my head with age-old plea
Please set me free
Can I be the real me?

Set Thou me free, set Thou me free
I pray to Thee on bended knee
Can I be free, can I be free?
I cling to my sanity
To be free is all I see

Release me from life's endless chains
And let me taste of Freedom's reigns
Fill the hole in my heart
Take my hand let us depart
To greater and greater plains

Hear me out
Destroy all doubt
Remove this pout.

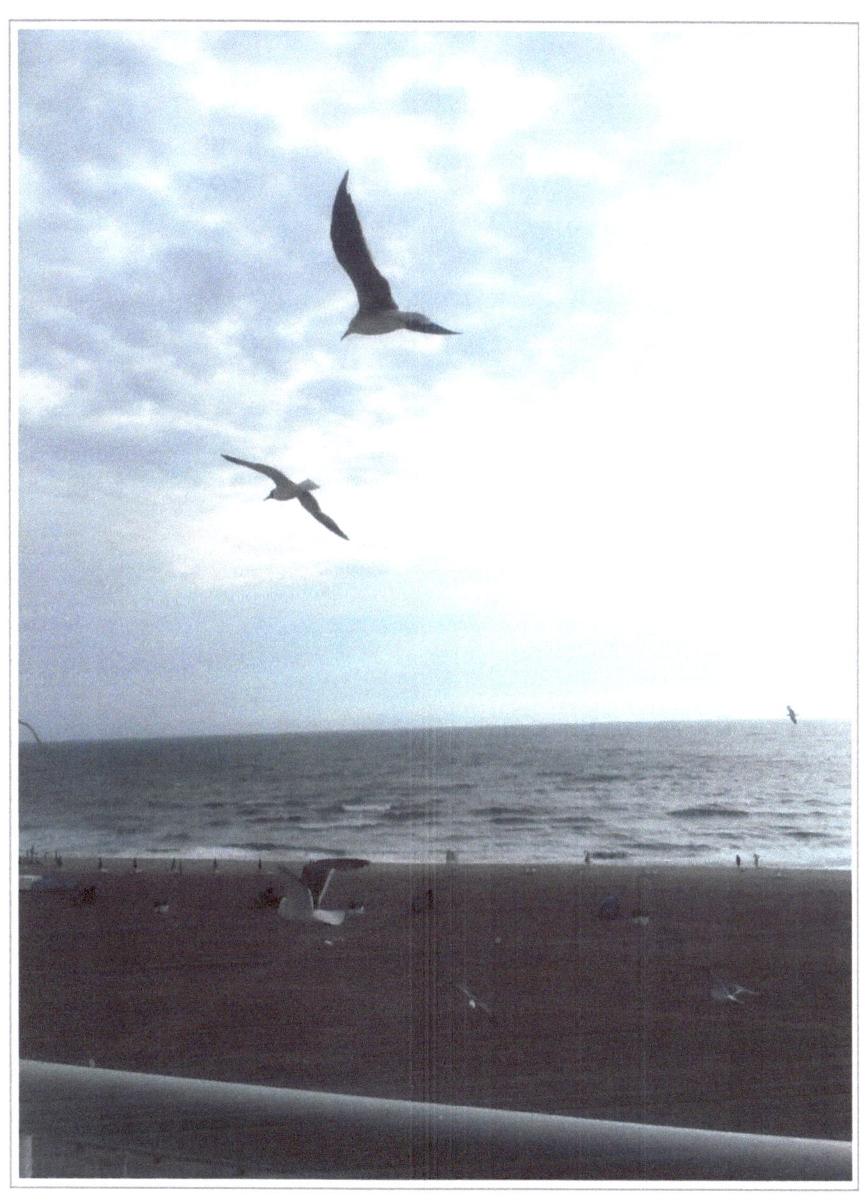

MOTHER NATURE

A gentle breeze blows
The beauty of a rose
The whisper of the leaves
And blossoms on the trees

A running river sings
A chirping bird now rings
Its tone so bright so shrill
Its flight above a hill

Mother Nature is the queen
She's the beauty of all scenes
And from whence she came can be
Hard to figure out you see

But her place is always there
From solid earth to invisible air
She whispers through the breeze

The river flows along
Constantly humming its song
Oh life what mystery
What divine harmony

Nature's course is sweet
So perfect and so neat
Though tales tell otherwise
Harmony beneath all lies

Mother Nature sing your song
Sing it clear and strong
For no foe can touch Thee
And destroy that harmony
Mother Nature, You're the queen

MY EYES WERE MEANT FOR THEE

In this world there is so much to see
In this world it's hard to think of Thee
Day by day, so many lonely cries
And that's why, my eyes
Were meant for Thee

My eyes were meant for Thee
My eyes were meant for Thee
There is so much to see
But nothing's there for me
My eyes, my eyes
Were meant for Thee

People search all over here and there
Where is love, can't find it anywhere
If they would turn their hearts and minds on Thee
They would find love everywhere

My eyes were meant for Thee
My eyes were meant for Thee
There is so much to see
But nothing's there for me
My eyes my eyes
Were meant for Thee

Thou art love and in our hearts You dwell
If we look within we'll find You strong and well
Direct our sight so that only You we'll see
And our eyes will be meant for Thee

My eyes were meant for Thee
My eyes were meant for Thee
There is so much to see
But nothings's there for me
My eyes, my eyes
Were meant for Thee

BATTLE

My passions well up inside of me
Threatening to take over
I ask myself if I can let go
Even for a moment
But I know the nature of my passions
You must be vigilant lest they destroy
Your holy ground and leave you desolate
Lost in a wasteland of hopelessness

Perhaps the key, then, is not suppression
But balance and tempering
Or perhaps, as the masters say,
It is to take charge and be in absolute control
Of one's own being, one's own senses
I know I stand not alone in this struggle
I know many others stand with me
Beside me, in front and behind
Facing the same struggle

I know that in the final analysis
It is up to me to choose
What will I settle for in my life
Fleeting willow-the-wisp joys
Or lasting hard earned happiness
I have decided that the latter is more desirable
But overcoming the habits I have formed
Chasing the tiny pleasures is difficult
They do not keep their promise

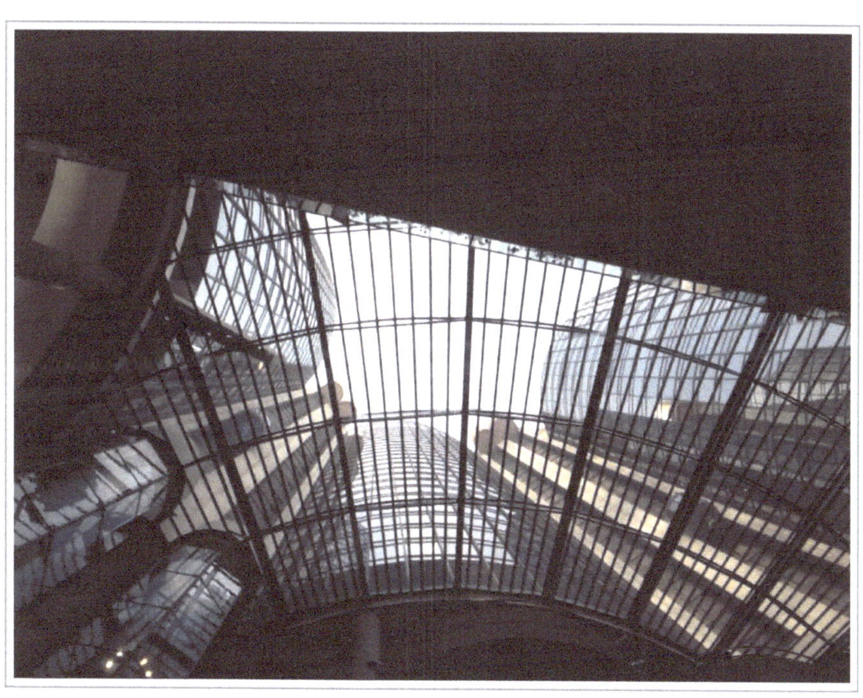

MY COMMITMENT

For so long I sought to quench my age-old thirst
From many tantalizing but empty wells
Even after repeated experiences
Of doubt, despair and disillusionment
Still after recouping from my disappointments
And healing somewhat
When confident again
And desirous of assuaging that age-old thirst
I would chase those same mirages expecting fulfillment

Through it all I had constant companionship and protection
Which in the throes of my indulgences,
I sometimes forgot
Through my experiences there was constant guidance by an
Invisible all-knowing hand
Finally, I am convinced that, in those invisible hands, lies the
Life giving water that I so desperately desire.

So I make my commitment to follow the way
That will lead me straight and fast
To the thirst-quenching well.
With haste and determination I will follow that narrow path.
I will take the road to freedom and to my beloved.
I will sacrifice on the altar of continued effort,
All things that stand a hindrance
The only hindrances are my own
Doubts and fears and self-created wants.

I've been so lost in trying to be something
I've been lost in trying to win
The approval of those around me

I've been lost trying to get love from man
I've been lost trying to prove my value to man
Wanting others to see value in me
Because of how I behave and act and what I do
I have condemned myself over and over
For not living up to this image that originates
Only in my own head's imagination

I've created ideas of what other people think I should be
And tried to live those ideas
Fully ignoring me and who I am
I've been successful in impressing others
At the cost of destroying my own happiness and well being
I've abandoned who I really am and denied self
Causing my own self-destruction.

So now I ask myself who, really, am I
What do I want to do
How do I really want to be and live in this world
What does that have to do with anybody else
How valuable are my ideas and thoughts
What will it take for me to honor myself,
My ideas and thoughts, me

When will I let go of those
That have nothing to do with me or who I am
Yet that influence my behavior?

In an instant all is gone and life changes for good.
Where will I be in that instant?
Where do I want to be?

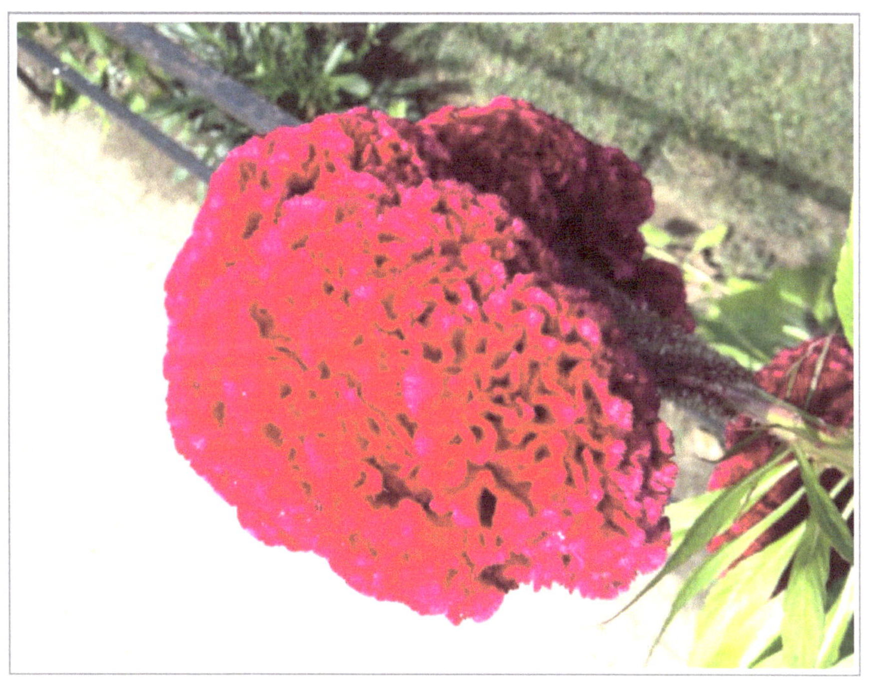

INHALATION

I inhale expectantly, hungrily, after having been starved for so long.
I crave a speck of anything that may look like joy or, should I say, bliss.

Initially, there is a temporary sense of relief and satisfaction as an encompassing feeling comes over me, yes it is pleasurable, but it carries other things with it and soon they take charge and the pleasure is only a memory.

But there is also a looming sense of fear that, seemingly, appears from nowhere like it, too, is waiting for me; I try to ignore the fear and it subsides for a second.

A rush of nervousness floods my body and being. My heart races and I become very conscious of the sounds around me. In cadence with the sounds, my mind begins to weave tales of terror, subtly and, at first, not so horrifying but as I inhale time and time again the intensity increases almost bringing me to a point of petrifaction-thoughts well out of control.

These thoughts-what are they and where do they come from? Why are they so persistent as they gain dominion over my mind. Soon I am so scared I can hardly breathe.

Everything seems loud and I think my breathing is perceptible and will be the cause of the terrible fate that awaits me so I try to breathe softly.

My mental efforts to control my thoughts become weaker and weaker. Soon I am helplessly horrified. Afraid of doing anything; afraid of being caught by those I love or by the authorities.

Maybe my fear is a blessing in disguise because it destroys the experience and rattles my body and nervous system.

Even after I am done the fear lingers and my mind still wonders about the people around me-what they think of me, can they perceive my imperfections? Are they silently criticizing me? Surely they must be. Yet even though I'm so afraid that I can hardly pick it up to inhale again or touch it lest I be caught, I don't want to stop I want to go on-two contradictory emotions taking me over.

I will not stop until I am forced by circumstances of one kind or another. Why do I put up with it?

After being away from it for a while and gaining some semblance of normality, after rebuilding my shattered pride and strengthening my mind and body, the desire slowly creeps in on me bit by bit until, finally, I rationalize doing it again.

I might fight the desire a little bit, but, eventually, I give in and go through the same harrowing experience again.

HIDDEN TREASURE

The hidden treasure that I seek
Lies not so close as to be revealed by a peek
Beyond sense lures, it lies, buried deep
Where only deep diving may yield its keep

The hidden treasure that I seek
Obscured by veils that may seem bleak
In reality, is the most unique
So much so that no words can bespeak

The hidden treasures that I seek
So humble it is, unostentatious, meek
Though man havoc he may wreak
Harmony it brings through ingenious tweak

Hidden treasures dazzling bright
Hidden by delusion's lesser light
Tear aside this affrighting veil
Show Thy face let love prevail.

ALONE

A fear grips my heart
as I consider the prospect of
moving away from you

It is a fear of not having you close;
a fear of not having your world blend with mine;
a fear of not having the preoccupation of your presence.

Alone I must face myself and my fears
There is no distraction of your presence
to keep my mind engaged

Alone I must look at myself
and my thoughts and my life
and decide whether I am satisfied.

Alone I must find out
whether I am lazy, bored, distracted
or just fear filled

Alone I am tasked
to bring meaning to my life,
to myself and my existence,

Alone I find out
whether I am sincere in my behavior
or whether I am putting on airs
to impress you
who have been so near for so long watching.

Alone I learn the great truths;
that I don't really know you
but imagine I do,
that I live in a fantasy world
where I create you
and your thoughts
and ideas about me.

A world where I imagine
there is comfort and security
because of your physical presence.

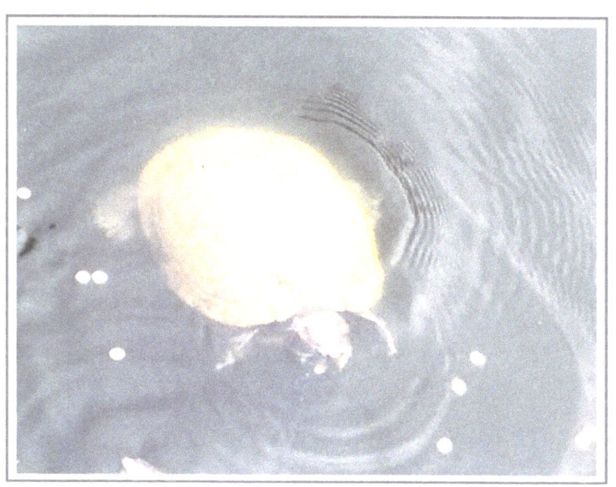

TO MY GURU

Oh My Divine Love
My Omnipresent Love
My Omnipotent Love
My God My Grace My Guru
I bow to Thee again and again

In Thine embrace I rest always;
Safe from any harm that may come
From dangers arm.
Thou walkest with me always
Watching me with tender care
Thou art always and forever there
Where else wouldst Thou be my Beloved?

Thou art mine and I am Thine
My heart can find no words
That adequately express my gratitude
For the attitude
Thou hast brought to this
Thine erring child

Thy child forever I am
And forever will always be
On bended knee I pray to Thee
Thou comest to remind me that
Thou are near, right here, and
On bended knee I need not pray
But arise and feel Thine embrace

Master, no words can truly say
What my heart feels and knows
I hope one day, I can be what You
Would want me to be
And I know it is happy, so very happy.

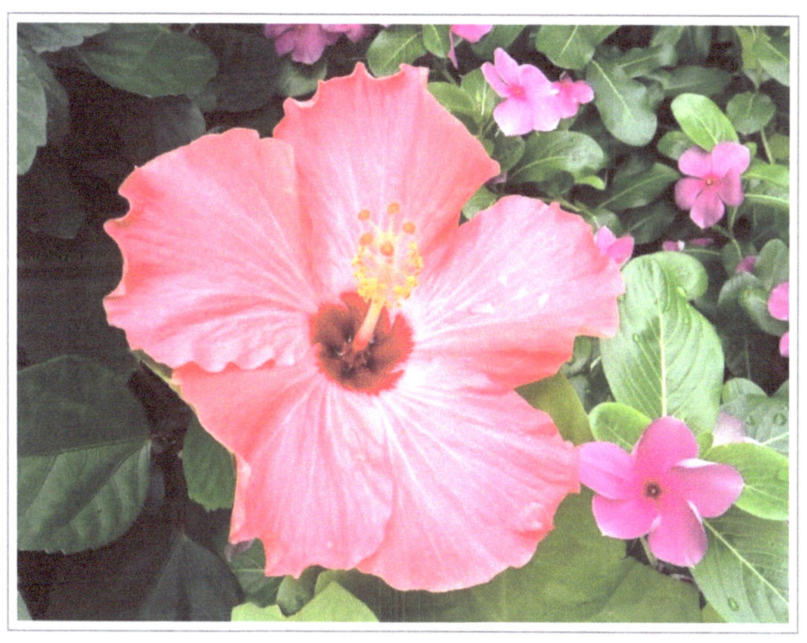

COME TO ME NOW MY LOVE

I love You as best as I can
And in my heart I know I can love You better
I know I have been temporarily way laid
By many willow-the-wisp of dead-end desires
But now my mind yearningly turns to Thee
Thou art the source of love
Thou art the goal I seek
Thou art the fulfillment I crave
Thou art the gnawing need of my being
I will transform all
My empty, meaningless, useless thoughts
Into the one aspiration to seek and find Thee now.
I will come after Thee with all the love of my heart
All the focus of my attention I direct Thy way
All my actions I dedicate to Thee
And I pray, I pray You come
And remove this veil of darkness
Come to me now, My Love, come to me now.

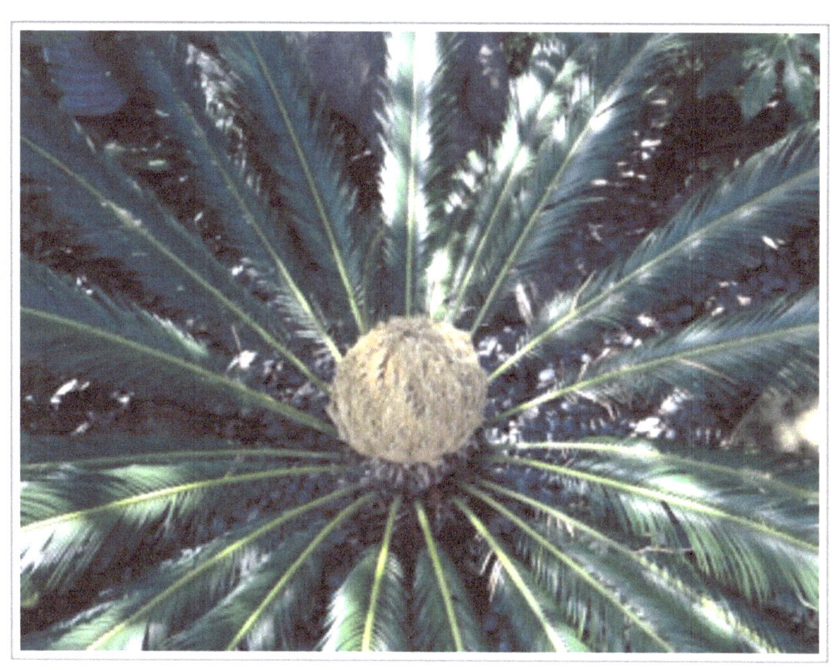

NO MORE

No more shall I prance around
In false pride and confidence
That I know some things,
Do anything,
Man anything
Without You

No more shall I drink from the glass
Of false pleasures and empty hopes

No more shall I desire anything less than You

No more shall I flaunt my so called knowledge,
I am as ignorant as ignorant can be

What do I know?

No more shall I flamboyantly show off anything
What on this earth have I created or made?
Nothing. Nothing at all.

No more shall I let
The seconds, minutes hours and days pass me by
In forgetfulness of Thee
And my freely chosen duty to love Thee.

No more shall I complain about anything,
All things come from Thee
And were created by Thee
For the sole purpose of helping to set me free.
Thou knoweth what I need
And bringeth it before me constantly
That I may have the great opportunity
To draw nearer to Thee quickly.

No more shall I let my wild mind
Feel lost or lonely when thou art right here with me.

No more shall I look at other men
In cold judgment and misunderstanding;
But for the grace of God there go I.
Have I walked even a centimeter in their shoes?

No more shall I be obsessed with anything
That reminds me naught of Thee
That brings not my attention
Humbly into the thought of Thy presence,
That places me not humbly at Thy feet.

A POEM A DAY

A poem a day
To keep boredom away
I will write my heartfelt lay
Day after day

A poem a day
Time's not wasted this way
When sentiments deep
Through my words do peep

A poem a day,
A window to my heart
A whisper of love
Inspiration to impart

A poem a day
To whisk lofty minds away
From dreary earth concerns
From fiery actions' burns

A poem a day
There is no other way
For me to say
I'm happy as a Jay

A poem a day
To soothe the heart and say
Why love is right here
Drawing ever near

A poem a day
With one purpose to relay
With outward garb array
My soul-felt gifts for aye!

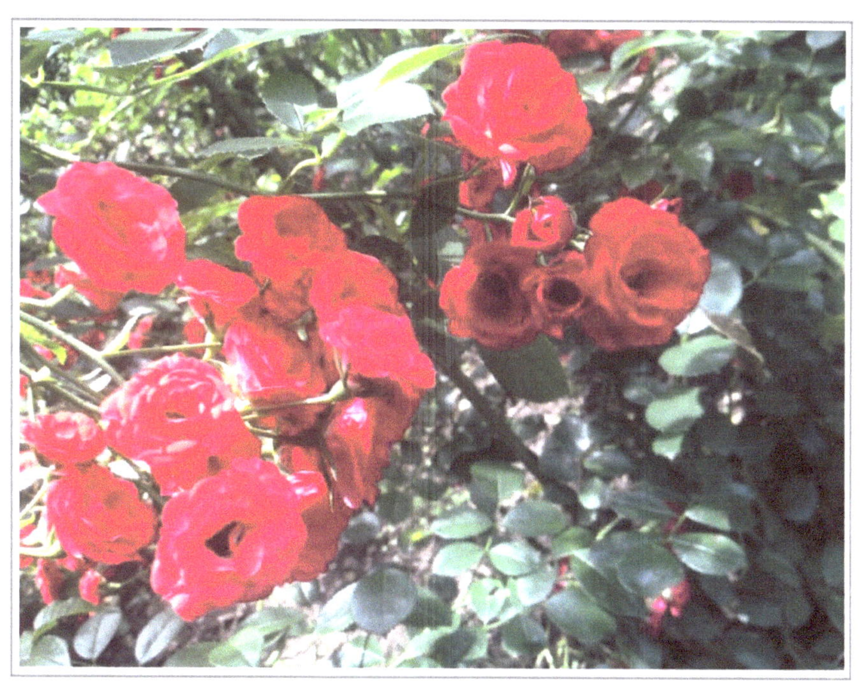

LABYRINTH

Every step must be considered
For every step yields a result
No man wants his future withered
By choice that's full of fault

So caution must be taken
And lessons must be learned
From darkness we must awaken
To pure light our hearts turned

Why travel a dark and winding path
That you know not where it leads
Why get lost in labyrinth deep
By unthinking and sullied deeds.

Why drown in falling darkness fast
Where monstrous passions feed
Why feel the effects of delusion's wrath
Yielded by uncontrolled sense steeds.

Escape the endless winding tunnels
That straight before you lay
Arise above grounds furnace funnels
To the blazing light of day

That freedom right here right now lies
Awaiting your embrace
Grasp it in fluid motion wise
All doubt must be erased

Take wing to higher and higher skies
Where labyrinth cannot you hold
Be glad with ignorance's demise
And watch your Self unfold.

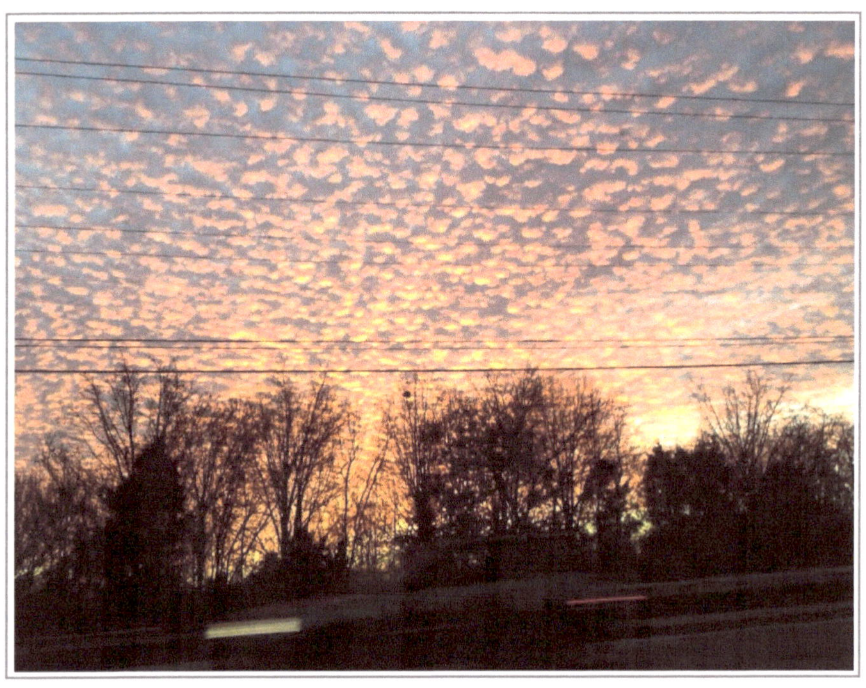

About the Author

Born in Accra, Ghana on 1st October, 1965, Kaggwa was uniquely endowed with a kind and gentle spirit coupled with joy and a playfulness that was arresting.

Around fifteen years of age, he discovered, "The Autobiography of a Yogi" by Paramahansa Yogananda and became a member of his organization, The Self Realization Fellowship. Its teachings and practices remained a driving force throughout his life.

Having maintained that he was from another planet, Kaggwa was a seeker of truth and believed that it could be found through self mastery, meditation and prayer. He avidly studied the lives of recognized visionaries and saints.

He left on 29 November, 2014.

APPENDIX

TO MY BABY

I love you now and always
With all my heart and soul.
I will look after you.
Whenever you fall
I will lovingly and softly pick you up.
Whenever you call
I'll be there in an instant
No one can hurt you
For I am your protector
I embrace you with my love and light
And shield your soul and heart against the night
Never will you fear a thing
For with me here always nothing dare touch or harm you
You can always talk to me and never be judged
Never fear to make mistakes
You are growing and learning
I love you so much
I feel and respond to your every need.
I give you my tender touch.
I hug; I embrace you
You are safe; you are sound; you are secure
You are beautiful, so beautiful!
You deserve only the best life has to offer
You deserve only pure, true love and happiness
You are protected and covered
And immersed in God's light and love
You deserve the best foods, abodes, friends,
But I will always be your constant, unchanging friend
In a world of treachery

Come to me, I will comfort and care for you.
I love you.
Relax and let go for you are safe and secure
And complete in my love
I love you. I cherish you.
I help you find your dreams.
I help you realize your goals.
I expect nothing from you.
I am happy with you exactly as you are now.
I love you now as you are.
Nothing you say, think or do will diminish
Or change that love.
It is always there for you-unconditional
You need prove nothing to me or anyone.
You are perfect as you are.

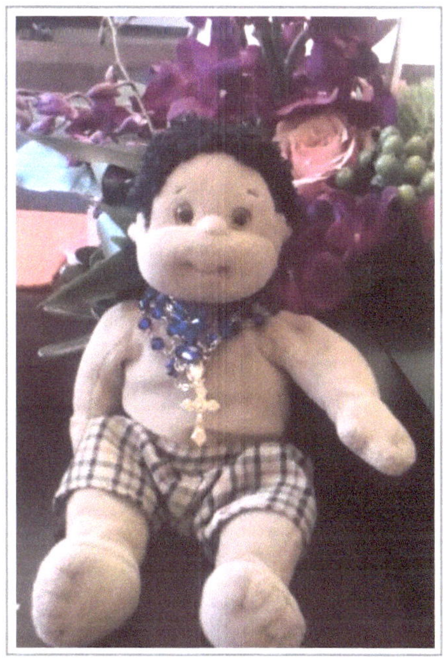

AFTERWORD

Love is one of the most misused words in the English language. In the misusing of it, we have weakened it and lost so much of the power that it can bring into our lives as well as the lives of those around us at any given moment.

The true essence of Love is intimate and manifested in ways seen and unseen although we are unable to fully comprehend or express it with words. My brother, Kaggwa Lubega, was a humble soul who introduced me to the deepest and most profound aspects of Love in such a way that, even though he is gone from my sight, I am still growing into the realization of its full value and meaning. Now, more than ever, I appreciate that the Love of which he made me aware is here guiding, supporting and protecting me in every instant. It is silent, it is sweet and it is the epitome of caring. Love was and is the embodiment of my dear brother.

This book is an ode to the Love he sought and bequeathed to every individual. It is Kaggwa's expression of gratitude to that Power which silently guides, protects and cares for all of us.

A River of Love!!!

With his dear words, he expresses his reverence for that Love and shares his appreciation with the reader, whisking all open hearts into his experiences so that each may realize, anew, the presence of Love in every moment of life. *Leo S.L. Lubega*

www.ingramcontent.com/pod-product-compliance
Lightning Source LLC
LaVergne TN
LVHW052253100826
845147LV00001B/34

* 9 7 8 0 9 8 6 2 3 2 2 2 0 *